Rugby: Body and Soul

MAINSTREAM *SPORT*

RUGBY
BODY AND SOUL

BILL SAMUEL

MAINSTREAM
PUBLISHING

EDINBURGH AND LONDON

MAINSTREAM PUBLISHING COMPANY (EDINBURGH) LTD
7 Albany Street
Edinburgh EH1 3UG

First published in 1986 by Gomer Press

This edition 1999

ISBN 1 84018 258 X

A catalogue record for this book is available from the British Library

Printed and bound in Finland by WSOY

Yn gyflwynedig i Velda fy ngwraig;
fy mhlant a'm hwyrion, gyda
diolch am wneud bywyd
mor ddedwydd

Acknowledgements

I would like to express my appreciation to my former colleagues and personal friends for encouraging me to write this book and to signify my gratitude to Cathryn Gwynn and Don Dale Jones for their advice and editorial skill. And to those innumerable typists, all of them beautiful, who laboured for the cause, thank you!

Contents

Foreword by Gareth Edwards   9
Introduction   11
One: The Joy of Being Poor   13
Two: The Law Brings Rugby to the Village   23
Three: The World of Work, Pranks and Play   36
Four: Infatuation with Rugby   50
Five: Rugby League or College Rugby?   62
Six: Branded Failures   76
Seven: Boy with Sporting Genius   88
Eight: From Tech to Millfield   107
Nine: Shared Achievement   121
Ten: Rugby Fever   136
Eleven: Giant-Killer   146
Twelve: Rewards   156
Thirteen: Decline and Fall of Welsh Rugby   165
Epilogue: The Changing Face of Rugby   171
Envoi   185
Index   187

Foreword

by Gareth Edwards

In my adolescence my ambitions, even though they were moderately pretentious, were associated with sport. That was until I met Bill Samuel and then my whole lifestyle changed.

To say that he had a profound influence in my formative years would be a complete understatement – for he dominated them. Once he recognised a talent in me he began to shape me into the image he alone saw in me. His authority, knowledge and experience were unquestioned.

I used to enjoy staying after school to be taught by him on a one-to-one basis. His prophecies, expressed to me confidentially at the time, made me blush, for they seemed unattainable. However, he built up my game and confidence to such an extent that when I eventually came under the direction of team coaches, at whatever level, they never bothered me, for they knew I had been taught to adapt my game to accord with any coaching contingency. In addition, I never sustained a serious injury playing rugby, which in itself is a testimony to my early training at Pontardawe: 'You must learn to play rugby with your brains and not with brawn'; 'Win modestly and lose graciously, that is the hallmark of a great sportsman'; 'Bide your time, you are entitled to break twice within a game. Make sure a try ensues from your efforts.' I can still hear Bill's words conditioning me for the big time. Not many shared his conviction. I often wonder what would have happened to me if good fortune had not blessed me with his presence.

Now that he has written a book I am looking forward to reading it with great anticipation, for I am sure it will be entertaining, thought-provoking, humorous, compassionate and written with a great deal of affection for the people of the Swansea and Amman Valleys. Bill is unashamedly Welsh, and I wish him well.

Gareth Edwards, 1986

I am glad that Bill's book has been reprinted and, like many others, surprised that it has taken so long. Famous rugby writers have over the years eulogised *Rugby: Body and Soul* as one of the best ever rugby books. There can be no better recommendation than that.

After all these years I continue to be grateful to Bill for preparing the way for me at Pontardawe Tech. His teaching of PE and of rugby football was simply marvellous.

Hwyl, a phob bendith Bil.

Gareth Edwards, 1998

Introduction

This book is partly about a way of life which has vanished now, that of the Welsh-speaking West Wales collier and his family in the Swansea and Amman Valleys. It depicts their unrivalled comradeship and their common bond in the adulation of sport and the stars of cricket, boxing, soccer and rugby, so remote from their own environment. It is a book about success and failure; losers and no-hopers; sadness and joy; high moral standards; the ambition to teach. It is a book too about the growth of rugby football from its rather comical beginnings in a small village in the '30s to its exalted position of the '70s, when Welsh rugby players were idolised as never before – the nation's pride and joy. The development of the game is traced from its grass-roots level, in schools and villages, through college sport, first-class rugby and home internationals, to the ultimate achievement of British Lions victories over New Zealand and South Africa.

From amongst the many excellent players of that time, one was to stand out and make such a contribution to the game that a statue of him was placed in the capital city of Wales. Many experts claim he was the best player they ever saw. What was it that was so special about Gareth Edwards? A keen enthusiast of soccer, his destiny was changed when he discovered rugby during his formative years. This book tells of the way in which that happened from my own standpoint, as the teacher who had the pleasure of discovering and then nurturing in the boy the talent that would bring him to the eyes of the world. Those who have enjoyed the career and success of Gareth Edwards and thought they had chronicled all of his story will be pleasantly surprised to discover a fund of untold tales.

It is also a book about the value of physical education and the valuable qualities it can instil. I hope it raises fundamental questions, such as whether coaching was responsible for the Welsh successes of the '70s. The glory and the demise of Welsh rugby are narrated from a viewpoint that may be considered unorthodox and controversial, but which offers a way ahead. Here is a combination of anecdotes – often hilarious – and memoirs which capture, I hope, some of the delight and enthusiasm I have experienced in living rugby football.

Bill Samuel, 1986

It was often said by a certain Swansea Valley Councillor, a collier by trade, that 'nothing but the best is good enough for Wales'. It seems that his vision was shared by the New WRU and New Labour, for, in 1999, Wales is to have a new multi-purpose stadium and is to host the prestigious Rugby World Cup competition.

Both of these caused debate in Wales, for the Arms Park was a prized monument to a glorious Welsh rugby history, whilst Wales as a rugby nation had lost its lustre and therefore should have retreated to nurse and solve its problems before embarking upon such a mammoth project as the World Cup.

But such debate did not defuse the spirit of the protagonists, Vernon Pugh, Glanmor Griffiths and the new WRU committee, who collectively appear to have the expertise and the enthusiasm to succeed. All Wales, and all rugby-lovers the world over, will wish Wales well in its endeavours.

What remains to be done is to produce a Welsh XV that can regain distant glories. It has been done before and it can be done again. We must not let our country down.

This book has been updated since its original publication in 1986 with the addition of a new chapter. But for a few minor changes, all the original text is as it was twelve years ago.

Bill Samuel, 1998

Chapter One

The Joy of Being Poor

The small village of Craig-cefn-parc is some seven miles to the north-west of Swansea, and two miles from Clydach in the Swansea Valley. When I was born there, in 1924, it was a totally Welsh-speaking village. English was the language of the classroom but Welsh was the language of the school yard, of the chapel and of the home. All the houses, with the exception of six council houses and six colliery-owned houses, were privately owned. They were inhabited by very proud and happy people who kept their houses and tended their gardens with loving care. The parlour was the best room in the house where the piano was housed and the best furniture kept. The polished table would have the family Bible placed on it. Inside our Bible were the names of Esther, Catherine, Thomas, Bronwen, Glenys, Dilys and myself, seven in all. Large families were common; next door had nine children and there was a family up the road who were sixteen in number.

Nearly all the men worked in the local colliery and you were deemed a man at fourteen in those days. Working in the colliery was the only way to earn a living and the men had no alternative but to produce the best steam-coal from the six-foot Graigola Seam, which was found in abundance underneath the village. Nearly eight hundred men worked there daily. No one in the village made a fortune, but the coal-owners did.

Men in their pride, with responsibilities for large families, gave their all, many ending their working lives prematurely, coughing coal or suffering some physical disability. No family was spared. My own grandfather and uncle were killed there, my father died of the dust and my brother Tom was severely handicapped after an accident at the age of nineteen.

The shrill blast of the colliery hooter was a common sound, bringing lagging spirits when miners were forewarned of an impending period of forced idleness, and joy and merriment when the hooter called them back to work. One admiring colliery-owner said of them, 'Ay, you can force them to stop working in the colliery, but you cannot starve them, for each one of them has a self-sustaining plot of land with a pig-sty, a poultry shed and plenty of fruit and vegetables in the garden to keep him going.'

There was only one public house, which was not excessively patronised. In fact, there was an undercurrent of resentment against such a place, for it was considered a weakness to partake of drink, and those who did were inclined to be frowned upon. The scant money that was earned was considered too precious to be wasted upon self-indulgence.

The Co-operative Society was situated in the centre of the village. It was judged to be an example of practical socialism, where the customers were encouraged to become members and to share the annual profits, which they called the 'dividend'. Every family wisely used its annual nest-egg to purchase luxuries which were unthinkable otherwise. It was my mother's proud boast that it was the Co-op's dividend that ensured our annual summer holiday at Aberystwyth.

If it was the Co-op that filled our bellies, it was the chapel that gave us inspiration. It was the place for spiritual guidance, the place where God lived. It was the focal point for recreation and learning; the Band of Hope, the concert hall for the choir, and the Gymanfa Ganu; the floor of the eisteddfod, and the stage for drama. The minister was the social-worker, the welfare officer and, more importantly, also the manager of the village soccer team and the promoter of the annual Sunday School foot races and 'kiss in the ring', the highlights of the Sunday School tea party. Not only was the chapel our spiritual home, it was also our Albert Hall. Without it we would have been lost.

The miners had every justifiable reason to complain that their circumstances were at a low ebb but the farmers, in comparison, were really finding it difficult to exist. I remember the women coming to the door in their aprons made from potato sacks, selling potatoes, swedes, eggs, chickens and farmhouse bacon streaked with lines of thin red meat. It was difficult to sell at the best of times, but to sell to a people who were nearly self-supporting was a task indeed. That was the kind of difficult and impoverished environment in which we lived. Little wonder, then, that we created an oasis of enjoyment in physical activity – although that, too, was not without its hazards.

The village had one major disadvantage. Because it had developed on the side of a mountain slope, the houses had been built on cuttings into the side of the mountain and had been placed at various levels, resulting in a scarcity of flat spaces on which to play a major game. Many soccer teams were started by enthusiasts, but unhappily their aspirations were shattered by the unavailability of a decent pitch. Delegations were chosen to speak to the district councillors, but to no avail. Over the years, one or two of the farmers had agreed to a short-term use of certain fields outside the village, but as soon as the texture of the grass began to fade, so too did the continuation of soccer in the village for that season.

But this did not dampen the spirit of the young men and boys and prevent them from playing football and cricket in their leisure time. As soon as they had bathed and eaten their meal after the shift at the colliery, they would be out to play on any available piece of ground. A football was a treasure and to play with it was a source of great enjoyment and fantasy. Any boy who had the good fortune to possess a football was assured of close friends while the leather on the ball lasted!

The miners loved cricket too and would play for endless hours in the summer months. They rarely played with a proper cricket bat because they could not afford one, but that did not prevent them from making bats out of waste colliery timber, and scraps of corrugated zinc sheeting would be used for wickets. To play with a soft ball would ensure the longevity of the homemade bat, but to play with a cork ball meant that a new bat would have to be made more often.

Children's games in those days were imaginative. It was natural for the boys and girls to play anywhere in the village without fear of being attacked or molested by wicked people. Innumerable games had been handed down by the elders, such as foxes-and-hounds, hide-and-seek, horses-and-jockeys, cat-and-dog, hook-and-wheel, hopscotch, whip-and-top, strong-horses, ball-against-the-wall, marbles, quoits with used colliery horse-shoes – too many to enumerate here. Girls' voices could be heard chanting as they skipped happily – 'Teddy bear, teddy bear, touch the ground', 'Black currant, red currant, raspberry tart' and so on.

The most popular winter evening game was foxes-and-hounds – the game could extend through the whole village. The rules were quite simple. Two mixed teams would be chosen depending on the number available; sometimes there could be twenty or more a side. Sides would be chosen – 'boy, girl, boy'. A boundary would be set and the 'foxes' released, which meant that they were to go into hiding anywhere within the agreed bounds. Once a 'fox' was caught he became a 'hound' and would join in catching the 'foxes'. The last 'fox' to be caught would be the winner. A second game would start with the 'foxes' in the last game becoming 'hounds'. We spent many a winter evening playing this exciting game until it was discovered that Ogwyn had won on three consecutive nights, a very rare achievement indeed. Then it was discovered that he had been seen on one of the evenings sitting in front of a roaring fire, drinking cocoa, whilst all the others were out shivering on the chase. This suspicion of dishonesty deflated our zeal for the game and I cannot remember ever playing it again.

One year we swam in the river in February. We felt able to do so because the surplus hot water which came from the colliery boilers made the water nice and warm. With our private parts hidden by a Spillers cotton flour-bag, which we called a 'cock rag', we swam in the warm water of the river. The water nearest to the surface was moderately warm, but below that level it was perishingly cold. When we had had enough, we ran across the railway-crossing to the boilerhouse to warm and dry ourselves in front of a flaming boiler-fire. The kind stoker provided us with old newspapers so that we could dry ourselves. Such escapades proved adventurous at the time, but when I nearly passed on with a severe bout of rheumatic fever due to what my mother called 'crazy behaviour', that was the end of the early spring swimming for me.

As far back as I can remember I was always passionately fond of playing soccer. We all knew about the affairs of the famous clubs of the English Football League. Arsenal was my particular favourite, and I would often be lost in dreams of playing for them. One of the most exciting memories connected with football was when we were sitting in the classroom in November. Our concentration would be broken by the shrill cry of a pig being slaughtered in a nearby household. This sound would cause a commotion amongst the boys, and the question in our minds was always, 'I wonder if Jac will give us the bladder?' Jac was the village pig-slaughterer – his side-line to being a collier.

When the school bell ended the day, we would rush to assemble outside the house where the unfortunate pig's blood was running down to the gutter. Jac had seen us. With apparent ease he turned the pig on its back and with a flourish he plunged and pulled his knife to expose the stenching innards. Then, with the dexterity of a Harley Street surgeon, his left hand disappeared to explore amongst the steaming flesh. A pause, a flick with the knife steady in his hand, and out came the glistening prize – the steaming pig's bladder. He squeezed it, and then, with an expression of distaste, he blew until the veins appeared to be bursting on his blue-scarred face.

'Who will burst first, boys, Jac or the bladder?'

Jac finally twisted the tube into a knot and with a kick from his hobnailed boot sent the bladder sailing on to the road.

'Hwre i Jac, bois,' we chorused as we kicked our newly found ball all the way home.

Whilst most of us were poor, Ossie was different. His father was in business and accordingly Ossie had everything. He was the only one dressed in proper football attire and it was he who supplied us with footballs and cricket gear for a number of years – those of us, of course, who happened to be in Ossie's gang. He ruled us with splendid superiority and woe betide anyone who crossed him, for it meant banishment from playing for quite a while. Such was his opulence that he could equip one group of boys with Red Indian clothing, bows and arrows included, and the other group with cowboy hats, holsters and six-shooters.

Depending on his mood, and this depended on his study of the previous week's comics and on how his heroes had fared, it was his choice to be Sitting Bull and his braves, or Jesse James and his gang. His inclination was frequently to go for Jesse James, since he claimed that Jesse was of Welsh descent. Whichever side Ossie chose, it was an unwritten law that he should win, and, for the sake of future games, it always transpired that he was alive at the end. Even if he were staggering, with smoke coming from his last shot, or with a broken leg and two shots in his back, Ossie would always pull the bow to send the final arrow to kill the last of the enemy. No one was allowed to outshoot Ossie.

Ossie was also a scientist and an avid reader of all the weekly comics such as *Rover*, *Wizard*, *Hotspur* and so forth, which his mother bought for him. In addition, he had, at the top of his garden, a laboratory which included a chemistry set of sizeable proportions. He liked to give the impression of being a scholar, and there he would lie, reclining on a settee, a packet full of sweets by his side, munching away and browsing through his comics. No wonder, then, that during the school holidays there would usually be a group of boys waiting outside Ossie's house.

At ten o'clock he would emerge, throw a glance at us and, with complete lack of acknowledgement, walk up the garden path to his exclusive laboratory. He would remain there, depending on his spirit, until he would appear and call, 'Teg, come up!' Tegwyn, who had been waiting patiently with the rest of us, would scamper quickly up the garden path into Ossie's domain. Ossie, casting his eyes over his minions and giving great thought, would also disappear. Again, depending on his mood, Ossie would repeat this same procedure every ten minutes or so until all the boys were in his lair. This daily routine made many of the boys bite their nails in anguish, and the last one suffered the most – as I knew very well from experience.

Once inside, one would find Ossie in the role of tutor, giving a summary of the exploits of his particular heroes from his complete stock of weekly comics. Most of us could not afford the twopence needed to buy *one* comic and I was grateful to our benefactor for introducing us to the characters in his comics. I found that I had a liking for sports stories, especially when the yarns had sports masters as heroes. I remember thinking at the time that being a sports master would be my ideal career when I grew up. Little did I know then that sport was going to absorb most of my future life.

The focal point in the village for discussion about sport was outside the chapel after service on Sunday evening. The older brethren used to gather there and discuss current political trends. Before the discussion ended, there would inevitably be opinions expressed on soccer, rugby, boxing and cricket. Although boys such as myself were present, *we* were not allowed to make a contribution to the discussion.

Some men thought that rugby was a foolish game and I remember being supportive of this opinion at that time. But when I grew older, I noticed that there was a difference in opinion regarding the merits of rugby and soccer. It seemed to me that those who were keen on rugby had either been to a grammar school or had sons or brothers who had played the game. And so it followed that there was a class distinction: rugby was for those who were more academically minded.

Was not rugby a gentleman's game invented by a boy in a famous English public school? Did not the two local grammar schools play it? Surely what was good enough for them was reason enough to adopt rugby as the game to play and follow? It was also evident to me that the followers of rugby in the group were far more eloquent and articulate than those who followed soccer, which was due probably to the fact that many of them would have been potential academics had they been given a chance earlier in life.

There was a difference of opinion, certainly, but there was no bickering or malice, simply pleasure. The youngsters listened agog to the exploits of the internationals at the Arms Park and to the stories of the great English soccer teams. It seemed impossible to us at the time that some of the villagers had really seen such wonderful moments in such rare places. We were full of admiration for their good fortune and enterprise.

Question: 'What was the longest punt ever recorded?'
Answer: 'When Lew James punted a ball into a coal truck in Clydach and it was carried to Swansea seven miles away.'
Question: 'Who played for England and Wales on the same day?'
Answer: 'The Gwaun-cae-gurwen Brass Band.'
Question: 'What team outside of England won the English Football Cup and never scored a goal?'
Answer: 'Cardiff City. Never was the name of the player who scored the goal.'

This type of indoctrination into the folklore of sport was fascinating, although not all the chapel members were in favour of sport and some were quite aggrieved at discussing sport on Sunday, especially with young boys like myself listening to every word.

In those days the famous St Helen's ground at Swansea used to share the home internationals with the Arms Park at Cardiff. It was said that Mr Morgan Havard, our chapel's precentor, used to look forward to each match at Swansea, not for the same reason as the others, but to listen to the pre-match singing. Once the ball had been placed on the halfway line to start the match, Morgan would be on the way home.

But I remember Morgan Havard for another reason as well. Like many boys, on Sundays I was sent to evening service – 'for you to learn something'. One Sunday night in particular, the chapel was packed with devout Baptists who had gathered in numbers to listen to one of the foremost preachers in Wales. All the boys, myself included, were sitting in the front row of the gallery, looking like angels but capable of wickedness at a moment's notice. We had eaten our long-lasting wine gums during the reading of the text, we had exchanged and read soccer, cricket and rugby league cigarette cards during the prayer and we were now playing tit-bit whilst the minister was immersed in a huge crescendo of evangelical spirit in his long-awaited sermon. The boys were becoming bored with playing tit-bit and with the minister's sermon and began to poke each other in the ribs with their elbows. Unawares, they were being watched by one person in particular, Mr Morgan Havard. The preacher's sermon was suddenly stopped by the booming voice of Mr Morgan Havard.

'Pardon this intrusion on your excellent sermon, Minister, but some of the boys sitting in the front are being naughty. Will you forgive me while I find my way to sit by them?'

There was a deathly hush in the packed chapel. Morgan, with great deliberation, moved to sit by us.

'Thank you, Minister. You may carry on now.'

We did not budge thereafter.

The big occasion of the year was the annual Sunday School trip to the seaside, which always seemed to be Porthcawl, Barry Island or Tenby. In those days the bus was the only mode of transport and the bus garage was in our village. The Baptists were proud to think that the Eclipse Bus Company's owners belonged to the chapel. Mr Phil Griffiths, one of the drivers, was our hero; he was our equivalent to Fangio or James Hunt. He was the driver of Bus No. 1 of the Eclipse Motor Transport Co. and, more importantly, *our* driver to Porthcawl on the Sunday School trip. Come the day, the three buses were to leave at nine o'clock sharp from outside the chapel, but the boys were in Phil's bus at eight o'clock, in the garage, some biting their nails in eager anticipation of the long drive to Porthcawl and the sea. Much to the boys' consternation, the two other drivers arrived earlier, and before long had started up their powerful engines and moved out of the garage and down the steep slope to the gaily costumed and eager throng waiting below. Nine o'clock came and passed. 'Where's Phil?' was the dismayed chorus. We *had* to be first in Porthcawl! The boys had disappointment, anxiety and tension written all over their faces.

'Here he comes!' someone cried. At once there was a bustle of excitement.

'Come on, Mr Griffiths! They'll be in Porthcawl before us.'

Phil's sturdy, tall figure walked without haste towards the bus, puffing a cigar with pleasure, his kindly red face beaming. 'Don't worry now, bois bach, we'll be in Porthcawl before them yet,' he said, with a knowing wink. Was it possible, after giving them fifteen minutes' lead? Phil's confidence was not wholly shared by his passengers. The powerful engine spluttered and then gained power; the bus moved out of the garage. Could he do it? Phil's face lost its smile and a grim determination appeared on it; he had changed his identity. He wrestled with his wheel, made many changes of posture and indicated by his movements that he was doing his best. The whole complement of boys remained silently transfixed. The intensity with which Phil drove encouraged us, for when he passed a vehicle we gave a rapturous roar – but there was no sign of the other buses.

Someone had the temerity to knock on Phil's window, only to recoil at the severity of Phil's facial expression. Three more miles to Porthcawl, the milestone indicated! When we came around a bend, there was Bus No. 3. Our hearts leapt as we passed it at full throttle. 'Hooray! Hooray! Well done, Phil!' Phil acknowledged the other bus driver by touching his brow with the hand that was holding his cigar.

He, somewhat dejectedly, responded with a faint smile. Where was Bus No. 2? Phil was still at it. Steam emerged now and then from his radiator. Was that a bad sign? 'Not far from the sea now, boys!' someone said. As he did so, there was Bus No. 2 in front of us, coasting confidently and comfortably towards the rapidly filling resort. With a last roar, Phil accelerated. We held our breath. The road was obviously too narrow. I closed my eyes and clenched my teeth, to hear a thunderous roar which could only mean that Phil had done it again. We were first!

When we got off the bus at the car-park we all rushed out to acknowledge our hero as he alighted from his cabin. One or two slapped him on the back in admiration. He was the master-driver, and we could only bask in his reflected glory. Phil, grinning broadly in his own inimitable style, raised his hand and continued smoking his cigar.

Many years later I discovered that Phil used to arrange that ploy with the other drivers in case we should be restless on his bus. I can now appreciate his psychology, but nothing could destroy those thrilling moments he gave to the boys of Elim Baptist Chapel, Craig-cefn-parc, on that never-to-be-forgotten Sunday School trip.

Chapter Two

The Law Brings Rugby
to the Village

One of the most scholarly gentlemen in our village was 'Noah'r Crydd', as he was affectionately called by the members of the community. He was a cobbler by trade, but he augmented his meagre living by tending his smallholding when there was a lull in the business. Noah was a prime example of an old Welsh tradition. He was steeped in the culture of Wales and could discuss the merits of poets and their work. He possessed wisdom and his own peculiar brand of philosophy, which earned him respect from a wide area. He was an intelligent man whose powers of argument and worldly knowledge were unsurpassed for a man who had left school at an early age. He was the brother of the poet Crwys, a man who was known as the Welsh working-man's poet and who won the most treasured of all prizes in Welsh poetry, the Chair at the National Eisteddfod of Wales.

As a young boy I used to take boots for him to repair. On occasions I would intrude on a gathering of some of his intimate friends holding a spontaneous religious service. Noah would signal for me to sit down in an unoccupied chair while the service continued. One of them would read from the Bible, another would pray and, finally, with great fervour, they would sing from memory all the verses of a favourite hymn.

Noah was partial to a glass of beer, a justifiable weakness, so he claimed, for it was in the local that he collected the debts for repairing shoes. 'You can't sit down in a pub without drinking a glass or two, can you?' he used to say defensively.

Noah had a major weakness which he shared with me. Hidden in his cobbler's shop would be copies of the American boxing magazine *The Ring*, which he used to purchase on his rare visits to Swansea and in due course would lend to me on condition that I read them thoroughly so that he could discuss current trends and stories of the boxing world with me.

His mouth full of small nails, he would clout the 'sprigs', as he called them, one by one into the leather and at the same time hold a conversation with me, while still clenching his teeth. Sometimes he got terribly excited when relating a particular fight. He would hammer the 'sprig' with as much ferocity as if he himself were giving a knock-out blow.

Noah loved boxing, especially the Welsh boxing heroes Tommy Farr, Jack Peterson, Jim Driscoll and Jimmy Wilde, and he never failed to speak of them with great affection.

Looking back upon that period now, it seems particularly carefree; above all else, there was that great gift of time to spend in talking, debating and watching others at work. As children, we made the most of the freedom for as long as we possibly could, although it did seem to hang in the balance upon occasions! I well recall the advent of a brand-new encyclopaedia to the household. I flipped the pages and read those about boxing, soccer and cricket, which satisfied my immediate curiosity, but thereafter it was with reluctance that I would stay indoors to read it. I was never keen on the words, only the pictures. At the time I did not appreciate the sacrifice my parents had made. My own philosophy at the time seemed sensible enough: I will study tomorrow.

The importance of the scholarship examination at 11+ did not register in my mind until it was too late. When the results were made known by the headmaster, and the successful children allowed to go home to convey the good news to their parents, I experienced, for the first time, a feeling of inferiority. It was too late to wish that I could make amends. The following Sunday, the minister warmly congratulated the children who had passed the 11+. I began to regret being present, but he was a man of compassion and worldly experience.

'Our commiserations to those who have failed. Let it be known that God in His infinite wisdom does not allow all the flowers to blossom at the same time.'

I look back sometimes at the education they gave children at that time in that village school and recall that it befitted a school in England more than one in Wales. Every classroom had a huge map of the world hanging on the wall, displaying in pink the countries of the Great British Empire. We were constantly reminded of its universal power, of which Wales was but a small part. Our history lessons were in praise of Clive, Cromwell, Drake, Henry, Wellington, Nelson, Cook and others of the same ilk. Our singing lessons would have delighted the most ardent English nationalist: 'Rule Britannia', 'God Bless the Prince of Wales', 'Land of Hope and Glory' and 'God Save the King'. The headmaster read beautifully, enthralling us with excerpts from *Tom Brown's Schooldays*, *Kidnapped*, *Black Beauty*, *Robinson Crusoe*, *Oliver Twist* and *Gulliver's Travels*. We had to learn poems which were also reverently English in flavour:

> 'If I should die, think only this of me:
> That there's some corner of a foreign field
> That is for ever England.'

> 'I must go down to the sea again, to the lonely sea and sky . . .'

> 'O to be in England
> Now that April's there.'

> 'There's a breathless hush in the Close tonight –
> Ten to make and the match to win –'

Without a doubt the poems made an impression on most of the children, for even to this day I can still remember the first lines of each one. The English language was such an irresistible force that even our punishments meant an extra dosage of it. We had to write out the following, for example, from five to ten times, depending on the teacher's mood:

> 'I presume that your presumption is precisely incorrect and
> that your diabolical system is beyond my comprehension.'

It is incomprehensible now that such emphasis was placed on the English language in the education of the children of the Swansea Valley. Despite the extensive use of English in the village school, however, Welsh retained its grip as the predominant language of the villagers, mainly because it was the language of their religion.

My education was to continue at the Clydach Central School, later to be called a secondary modern school. It was there I came across rugby football.

The games master was under the illusion that the Graig boys were virtually hill-billies and gave us an old tattered football to kick around in our games lesson, while he supervised the other boys playing rugby. The only occasion I remember playing rugby was when I made a fleeting run with a rugby ball during lunch-time, until Ernest, a farmer's boy from the Graig, ripped my blazer in half. I was stunned, and nearly in tears, for the blazer had been handed down to me by my cousin, Wil, who was at the grammar school. My mother cried when she saw the torn blazer. The following day I was back in school in my favourite well-worn jersey, happy as a sand-boy.

Teachers were held in great reverence. Their words and deeds were sacrosanct. One teacher in particular, Miss Hughes from Penclawdd, who taught English, had a profound effect on me. She had the ability to awaken the curiosity of the class and to convince children that learning was a happy and useful process. There is a saying in education circles that nothing has been taught until it has been learnt. Miss Hughes had that gift and even to this day I remember some of her lessons – the hallmark of a good teacher. If ever you need to know how good a teacher is, do not ask the headmaster, ask the children. They are the only true judges.

Once home from school I found that I had lost many of my former friends, for they had become occupied with the homework which was part and parcel of a grammar school education. But that was not the only reason. A few of the parents of the scholarship children made it perfectly plain that their clever sons were not to fraternise with boys who were without brains, such as myself. This ostracism made me realise that certain people did not want to recognise losers and that the stamp of failure could be a blemish on one's personality for ever.

For a time, therefore, I retreated from the main play areas, until those of us who were in the same boat discovered that failure could be more interesting than success. Whilst the clever boys kept their heads down at night, chained to a chair, poring over books, we were on the rampage, playing with coal trams and trucks on the colliery surface; helping the Co-op's delivery man to take goods to outlandish farms by cart and horse; delivering evening papers; running messages; helping the farmers; fishing and swimming, and playing soccer and cricket to our hearts' content.

It was at this time that rugby came to the village of Craig-cefn-parc in the person of a new village policeman. His arrival caused a bustle of excitement, for he was none other than J.H. John, the ex-hooker of the world-famous Swansea Rugby Club, and an ex-international too. When it was announced that he was calling a meeting in the hope of forming a rugby team it was generally admitted that the man undoubtedly had vision. But to kindle the rugby flame in the village at that time seemed impossible, for there was no tradition, no ready playing-field and, more dauntingly, no players except for those few boys who played rugby at the grammar school.

I was at that inaugural meeting in Evan Hopkins's small general store and barber shop. I was about twelve at the time and full of curiosity about our new policeman and, to me, the foreign game of rugby football. The historic gathering was held in the storeroom, where Evan was busily cutting the hair of a customer. Since the only chair was occupied in Evan's transaction of duty, the enthusiasts – and they were not many – sat on a selection of flour, mixed corn, barley, bran and potato sacks.

The local schoolmaster was appointed secretary, and he remarked philosophically:

'I must confess that good fortune has really been kind to us in sending such an able and distinguished police officer to our midst. We are grateful not only for your presence, PC John, but also for your power as a policeman, for you can, by virtue of your position, open doors to us which have been closed, especially with those farmers who do not allow us the use of their fields.'

There was a chorus of agreement as the secretary sat down. J.H. hastened to assure them that everything would be done according to the law. True to his promise, during the forthcoming week he organised a group of young men to go into the woods of a private estate to saw down pine trees of appropriate length, all of which was done quietly under the light of the moon, and the timber taken with great care to be hidden in a safe place in the village. When the farmer discovered his loss, he hastened to report the matter to J.H., who sympathetically assured him that investigations would be made at once to find the rogues. When news of this incident filtered back to the small band of followers, J.H.'s stature rose considerably.

His next task was to find players, and this proved to be a different problem. He went around the village searching for young men, assuring them that experience or knowledge of the game was completely unnecessary. The response was minimal until he eventually found his way to the colliery's blacksmith's shop. It was there he found young men who shared his enthusiasm. His good luck continued, for they provided him with names of those who worked underground. With his police notebook and pencil at the ready, he waited for them to surface and then, with the aid of a companion from the blacksmith's shop, J.H.'s list was extended. Later on he cunningly invited two boys from the grammar school to play at half-back. This done, his list was complete and at last, so he thought, things were taking shape.

As the news spread in the village, J.H. and rugby became a talking-point wherever a group assembled, be it at the Co-op, the colliery or after evening service.

'What position did J.H. play?' one asked.

'He played hooker!'

'Was he any good?'

'Any good, you nitwit! He has played against the might of England, Scotland, Ireland and France.'

'He must be a tough nut, then!'

'Yes, popular and much respected. Fancy the great Swansea Rugby Club giving him a rugby ball so that we can practise. The boys must be raring to go!'

Yes, indeed, there was enthusiasm from the impatient lads who wanted to handle the ball – some of them for the first time. Mr Ford, the secretary, and Evan Jones, the treasurer, not to be outdone, organised a weekly raffle in the hope of acquiring, in due course, a set of jerseys. However, the problem of finding a suitable rugby pitch had yet to be resolved. It presented a major obstacle to the future development of the game in the community. In the meantime, the village school's shelter, which in fact was not much bigger than a boxing ring, was to be used as a gymnasium.

It was there, under the miners' carbide lamps and candles, that J.H. tried to teach the rudiments of forward play. They had come in their rough flannel shirts and hobnailed boots, the biggest, clumsiest and strongest set of lads in the village, some of them having cut and filled that day, with the help of a mate, ten tons of coal, or wrestled with hot iron at the forge for eight hours. They were determined to have some fun and they responded to J.H.'s teaching with a spirit that was so crude it nearly drove him to despair.

Some of the forwards had not shaved, and those who were soft-faced suffered considerable discomfort at the chins of the older wags. Now and again there would be screams of pain as a wandering hand would squeeze an unsuspecting pair of testicles. There were no supporting belts worn in those days, as far as these poor innocents were concerned. They pushed and wrestled, pulled and resisted until the sweat flowed from their brows. In the process, some of them revealed backs which were dirty from the dust of the colliery. It was a custom in the homes of miners during those difficult days, before the arrival of the pit-head and the domestic bath, to bathe in a zinc or wooden tub in front of the kitchen fire. On the Saturday, the last day of the week at work, they would have a thorough bath from head to toe with the added luxury of having either the wife or one of the children to scrub and wash the blackness away.

No one could complain of their effort to master the rudiments of rugby, for they were genuinely doing their best, but ignorance is a strange bed-fellow: J.H. was giving them gems of rugby information but none of it seemed to be retained, and he soon realised that he had undertaken a very difficult task. However, he showed his rugby international mettle by not giving in, not immediately, at any rate. But he was plagued by the incessant high spirits of the lads.

Bertie was a character who enjoyed a wicked sense of humour. A huge young man who worked with him suffered from what the colliers bluntly called 'the piles'. In Bertie's opinion he had the size to play for Wales but, as with most big men in Wales, was too gentle. To Bertie's mind this young man needed 'gee-ing up'. He had slyly poured some Sloan's liniment on the palm of his hand before the practice had started, and had waited his moment in the scrum before he applied his hand to his giant friend's tender area. Bertie had not reckoned, however, on the consequences of his prank. The young man was transformed instantly into a figure charged with electric current. He dashed from the shelter, hopping up and down the yard, bent like a sickle, clutching his posterior, in a state of absolute frenzy and shouting, 'Water! Water! The dirty bugger! Water! Water!'

J.H. stood transfixed for a moment before he, alone of the group, had the good sense to get the trainer's bucket of water and, pulling down the young giant's shorts, to splash his rear with a saturated cloth of cold water. It was some time before the pain abated, while J.H. stalked round the shelter, obviously in a rage, whilst the others remained unmoved, with their heads bowed in shame (or so it appeared) because of Bertie's diabolical trick.

J.H. threatened to finish rugby training there and then. 'You have let me down!' he said, fiercely. 'This cruel act we have just witnessed shows what wicked thoughts some of you have in your minds. Rugby is a tough, rough game played by gentlemen for fun. I'm giving you just one more chance.'

Much to everyone's surprise, Bertie restored the morale of the group by magnanimously accepting the blame.

'How was I to know that the liniment would have such an effect? I heard that some first-class players playing for Swansea did the trick, and in all innocence I thought I would try it for a bit of fun. I honestly did not believe that Wil would jerk, dance and scream as he did.'

This confession and the apt description relieved the tension and caused everyone to burst into uncontrollable laughter, with J.H. eventually joining in.

At the next meeting of the embryonic rugby club, a little dissension arose.

'Mr Chairman, I think we are putting the cart before the horse,' said Jonathan Thomas, one of the committee members. 'You are training our boys, running a raffle to get jerseys and have managed to get a ball, and yet we haven't got a pitch to train or play on.'

There were plenty of straight talkers on the rugby committee, but the forthright approach in this instance was questioned. Not only was J.H. the chairman, he was also the village police officer, and his motives should not have been questioned in this way. Some members thought it disrespectful to doubt J.H.'s wisdom. But J.H. had a practical suggestion in response. 'What about Mynydd-y-Gwair for training?' he asked. There was a gasp of astonishment at this suggestion. 'Mynydd-y-Gwair! But the Death-Ray Man lives up there.' J.H. observed the protest, but enquired reasonably, 'Can you think of another place?'

Overlooking the village at 600 feet was the mountain called Mynydd-y-Gwair, and on it a mysterious scientist had settled, a West Country man by the name of Grindell Mathews. He had flown over West Glamorgan in a monoplane to find a lonely spot where he could be sure of space, secrecy and privacy, and Mynydd-y-Gwair provided all three. His arrival there in 1934 quite naturally stirred the curiosity of the people of the village. What were his plans? They were soon to find out. Forty local men were engaged to work on the mountain to build a bungalow and a laboratory. At the mention of the latter, people began to entertain extravagant fantasies of awful scientific experiments. But it was discovered later that Mr Grindell Mathews was simply a scientific genius who wanted a quiet place in which to work. He was involved in defence experiments, and he wanted Britain's defences to be impregnable against the war-mongering Adolf Hitler. He was world-famous as an inventor, having already led the world in pioneering the radio-telephone, talking films, aerial mine-fields and death-rays.

He had surrounded his compound with high-standing posts and wire which could be electrified at a touch of a button. It was said that his mission was to produce a death-ray. A strange coincidence occurred when, for no apparent reason, motor cars came to a stop on the lonely mountain. The car bonnets would be raised and the engines examined but no mechanical fault could be found. Many an exasperated motorist discovered that, for some inexplicable reason, after a thorough examination the engine would start spontaneously. When these stories were conveyed to the villagers they were convinced that it was the work of the Death-Ray Man.

Obviously, therefore, the committee members were reluctant to support J.H.'s proposition while the famous and bizarre scientist was in residence on the mountain. Artfully persuaded by J.H.'s words, however, they gradually relented.

31

It was a sunny Saturday afternoon when they assembled at the foot of the mountain to ascend to their elevated pitch at 600 feet. They had changed in the open shelter of the school and a motley crowd they were; some had managed to procure proper rugby kit, but in the main the outfit they wore was a mixture of work and cast-off clothing. In contrast, the two grammar school boys, Enoch and Maldwyn Davies, looked neat and dandy in their school colours.

The jokes went round as they began their way gently up the gradient. One or two had to stop now and again because of unfitness and the need to light up a cigarette. When they got to the top, there was J.H., like Moses, breathless and nearly speechless, perspiration on his brow, surveying the top of the mountain, waiting for his aspiring protégés and at the same time throwing furtive glances towards the compound of the mysterious scientist.

The bounds of the pitch were set and coats stacked tidily to act as goalposts. The trial proved hilarious. The exchanges were reminiscent of a brawl. The few rules some of the players knew were soon forgotten. They jumped on each other's backs, like jockeys, in a crude attempt at tackling. Others would stick a foot out to prevent someone passing by. Howie flung the ball forward with all his might, shouting at the top of his voice 'Charge!', much to the exasperation of J.H., who was trying to referee the game. It was painful to watch and, for the first time, the dawning realisation of the enormity of his task was apparent on his face.

There were ant-hills here and there on the mountain surface, which caused many a player to fall headlong, but when J.H. stumbled and fell head-first on to a live ant-hill, the play stopped instantly. J.H. was in a torment, windmilling his arms around his body in an attempt to clear the innumerable ants which were causing him such discomfort. As he bellowed and danced around, scraping ants from his face and body, the players could not refrain from laughing. Alas, when J.H. finally cleared himself of the ants, he was a changed man. He had had enough and stormed his way from the makeshift pitch down towards the village in a huff. Some of the more responsible members of the group realised that J.H. had been really offended, so they dashed after him to mollify their mentor. By the time they had arrived at the school shelter to share the only pan of hot water, J.H. was already planning the next move.

That was a memorable day in the life of the village, when the game of rugby was introduced to the young men of the village of Craig-cefn-parc on a mountain cloaked in scientific mystery, in the proximity of an ominous, high, wired electrical fence, with mournful sheep as spectators and multitudinous skylarks providing the singing. It was no surprise to discover later that the village XV had been nicknamed the 'Death-Ray Stars'. I remember the Death-Ray Stars playing against the neighbouring village of Felindre. A local derby was to be played on Christmas morning on a makeshift rugby pitch specially made for the occasion. The game had come about because of the intense rivalry at the colliery with the two factions claiming superiority in the playing of the game.

It was a cold, frosty winter's morning when my brother Tom and brother-in-law George, on holiday from Surrey, walked the four miles across the wild, open countryside to the pitch. As we moved along, other supporters from the village joined us, and soon a crowd of us had gathered on the pitch and were admiring the painstaking way in which the Felindre boys had managed to acquire posts and sawdust for the various lines on the marshland where the game was to be played.

The teams had begun to change near the hedgerows and were busily tossing their clothes on to the frost-covered trees. They were all shivering, blowing their hands and rotating their arms in order to keep warm. When the teams were nearly ready to take the field it was discovered that the Death-Ray Stars' outside-half had not turned up. This annoyed J.H. Loyalty, honesty and punctuality were some of the qualities he had preached, and to be confronted with an off-the-field problem had not occurred to him. What was he to do now? He had no reserves.

The players stood around until they were blue with cold. When the culprit finally came, fifteen minutes late, J.H., with considerable control, gave him a stern lecture. To make matters worse, it was discovered later that the already out-of-favour outside-half had left his shorts at home. The chairman was exasperated and, with considerable impatience, chastised the outside-half at the top of his voice, at the same time desperately enquiring if anyone had a spare pair. But no one could oblige.

This predicament deflated J.H. temporarily but, much to his joy, the player decided to play in his underpants. Most colliery workers in those days wore long johns, and many a curious glance was cast his way when he walked in his new-fashioned short-legged pants towards the pitch, holding on to the front of his shorts to prevent any exposure of his private parts. Joking voices and laughter accompanied his arrival on the field of play. Such was the importance of the game, it appeared, that this inconvenience was not going to interfere with his enjoyment or his loyalty to his club. This was the feeling he conveyed to the Graig supporters, who were only too ready to show their admiration with applause.

He was the focus of all attention as he placed the ball on the sawdust halfway line and signalled with his free hand that he was ready to kick, while still clinging firmly to his shorts with the other hand. He kicked the ball to start the game and brought a roar of laughter from the crowd at his one-handed action.

The game was long remembered, not so much for its quality but for the sheer brilliance of the outside-half. His running from the scrum and lineout was completely unorthodox. One hand held his pants as he ran to take the ball, two hands were employed to take and pass the ball, but at this moment the fly of his shorts would release its contents. Then there would be a hurried fumble to return his embarrassment to the fold. This was his task throughout the game, and there was great amusement as he stuck manfully to it. Can you imagine Cliff Morgan, Barry John or Phil Bennett under such pressure at the Arms Park?

This spirit prevailed until the Graig supporters realised that the game could be won and became very serious. They suddenly became anxious and began cheering and willing their team to win. The outside-half had taken no part in the game except to link with his backs because he was so occupied with his own private concerns. With a few minutes to go and the Graig losing, as good luck would have it, the outside-half received a splendid pass from the base of the scrum. This time, with two hands on the ball and contrary to his previous game, he dummied beautifully, to the surprise of the defenders, his own players and supporters alike. Quick as a flash, with privates dangling and swinging in the frosty air, he ran through to score.

This magnificent contribution made him an instant hero as he returned, smiling, to his own half. He was acclaimed as the great gladiator. Someone aptly called him McDangle. There were two heroes above all others who returned homewards to Christmas dinner that day. He was one; J.H. was the other. When one reflects on J.H.'s contribution to the welfare of the young men of Craig-cefn-parc, one recalls the wisdom of his leadership. By involving himself with the activities of the young men, he was assured of their co-operation in maintaining law and order in the village. In this way, he was a natural forerunner of community policing. It was the secret of his success.

Chapter Three

The World of Work, Pranks and Play

When, at fourteen, the time came for me to finish school, I knew my next step was to find a job in the colliery. Because my father had lost his health, many socialists used to come to the house and have long discussions about the idealism of fundamental socialism, to which I used to listen with great interest. One of them had been to Russia and another to the war in Spain. They spoke about the inevitability of the nationalisation of the coal mines, the four-day week, the seven-hour day and, finally, with great hope, the removal of gases from the mines without the necessity for men to go underground at all. That notion was too far away for my own benefit. I had no alternative but to seek a job in the colliery. It was granted to me by the manager, the affable David John Price, Esq., ME.

The Clydach Merthyr Colliery was unique in one particular way. It was the only colliery in Great Britain that had coal-fired boilers underground to provide steam for the power to work the haulage engines there. This also meant that the miners could use carbide-fired lamps underground without fear of a gas explosion. I finished school on the Friday and started screening coal on the following Monday. It was, to say the least, a dirty and boring occupation. Hours would be spent in semi-darkness because of the intensity of the coal dust. We would pick up stones from the conveyor and drop them into a coal-truck which stood motionless below. We used to wear homemade masks made out of empty cotton flour-bags to cover our nostrils and mouths, but one thing was for sure: we would go home like the Black and White Minstrels after the shift had finished. One would work consistently during most of the day, but enjoy quiet spells when there was no coal to be screened. This was the time when one was able to discover what jobs the other lads were doing.

There was a natural progression from one job to another until one attained a certain age, and then, according to one's inclination, one had the choice of going to work underground or staying on the surface to learn a trade by going into the blacksmith's shop as a blacksmith's striker. The physical aspect of this job appealed to me and I bided my time.

My parents were still unhappy that I was working in the colliery and managed to find a job for me at the village Co-op as a shop assistant – a job which I really enjoyed. In those days a job in the Co-op was considered to be respectable and secure and offered advancement, but I did not stay very long because the wages were pitifully small.

I returned to the colliery and found myself working in the blacksmith's shop, thus realising a previous ambition. The boys who worked as strikers were really strong in the upper region of the body. I began to wield a seven-pound sledge-hammer daily, which afforded me great satisfaction, and I got stronger every day.

During the day the topic of conversation was rugby football. It was rugby all the time. I did not share their enthusiasm at the time and felt somewhat out on a limb. Most of them had played rugby or were current players, and the fitters and strikers made it perfectly clear that soccer, the game I played, was considerably inferior to rugby, the national game of Wales.

I played goalkeeper for the village soccer Under-Seventeen XI in the Swansea and District Sunday School League. My parents objected to my playing because there were two ex-soccer players in the village who had become invalids because of their association with the game.

For those who worked in the colliery at that time and who wished to play either soccer or rugby, it was a day full of activity. Work would start at 5.45 a.m. on Saturday, and finish at 1.30 p.m. Then would follow a mad dash to bathe in front of the kitchen fire, a quick lunch and then either catching a bus to play away or staying in the village for a home game. We always played our home games either on a farm or on marshlands outside the village. There were no facilities, just one bucket of hot water for both teams in the backroom of either the Masons Arms or Willie Evans's, the newsagent.

The village Under-Seventeen side was very good, but there was one team in the league which was exceptionally good: Tower United, from the Town-hill area of Swansea. The team contained no fewer than seven ex-Swansea schoolboy internationals. I remember one boy in particular playing against us at left-back, who eventually became the most highly priced footballer of his day. Even then, he was all-action, fiery and explosive; a cut above all those players around him. He played for Swansea in the early years of the war, scored his first hat-trick for them in the season 1944–45 and scored 24 goals in the same season. In 1946 he scored 41 goals and was transferred to Aston Villa for £10,000 and in 1950 he joined Sunderland for £30,000. 'Whenever he scores a goal, it's something to talk about,' the critics said of him. He was a two-footed marksman who was seen at his best in the red shirt of Wales. The Graig boys were quite proud of the fact they had played against Trevor Ford, even though it was when he was on the bottom rung of the ladder.

Another player from Swansea who used to guest for the 'Graig' was the late Bobbie Daniel, who is considered by many, even to this day, to be supreme among the Swansea products. He was snapped up from under the noses of the Swansea officials by Arsenal, but sadly he lost his life in World War II.

It was in a home match against Tower United that I made a blunder of which some of my team-mates remind me bitterly even to this day. All players, whatever their ability, play the game with the same dedication as top-class players. Winning is important at all levels; losing narrowly, because of an error of judgement or carelessness by one player, can result in a lifetime of recalling the misfortune.

Our soccer team existed because our minister of religion, the Revd Trevor Williams, BA, BD, and the secretary-player, Haydn Bowen, made up the committee and they made sure we behaved ourselves. 'Don't let the minister down, boys,' we were constantly reminded. We were too poor to have a kit. The team wore white shirts and, as goalkeeper, I wore a homemade jersey given to me by Dai

Bodycombe, the captain. I was having a busy time that afternoon against Tower United. During one save I hurt one of my fingers and swore, to compensate for the pain. Unbeknown to me the minister heard my words and demonstrated his displeasure by moving out of earshot.

The score remained blank at half-time. The home players walked away from me, for some of them had heard me swearing. The captain was furious and told me so. However, he was wise enough to rally us all and convince us that we could win the match. We scored a goal with about ten minutes to go. Later on I committed a grave error by kicking wildly at the ball and missing it, to allow a simple goal which drew the match. 'Don't let anybody down!' Our supporters made it known to me that I had thrown the match, despite the fact that I had saved what appeared to me certain goals.

The Revd T.R. Williams was certainly cross with my two misdemeanours, and some members of the team, too, were really annoyed. Hardly any members of the team spoke to me the following week, and the inevitable happened – I was dropped. I was given a private hearing by Revd Williams and Dai, the captain, who pointed out the error of my ways; giving a goal away was acceptable, but to swear in a Sunday School League game was abominable. I apologised in a very clumsy way and promised to mend my ways.

As it transpired, they played the same team away and lost handsomely. It was no surprise, but a personal relief, to discover that I was being recalled for the next match.

I loved soccer, but at work, whenever there was a free moment, rugby continued to dominate the conversation. My colleagues would talk endlessly about international rugby stars and famous games, of the exploits of first- and second-class rugby clubs, and would provide an incessant stream of personal anecdotes and experiences. These conversations proved to be my daily indoctrination for the next few years. My indifference to their ramblings made me an oddity in that company.

Over the years the blacksmith's shop had developed a tradition for playing practical jokes on newcomers. They tried them on me on various occasions: 'Go to the stores and ask for a sky hook; Brasso to clean the tram-rails; a left-handed spanner; a rubber sledge-hammer; a square wheel'; and even 'Go to the screening plant to fetch a wheelbarrowful of coal dust'. One could not afford to relax for a moment, but one day when I was off my guard I was caught by their cunning.

We were sitting on a large tool-chest discussing (quite harmlessly – or so I thought) the question of strength. Tom Inch came under review, as did Charles Atlas, local strong men revered for their feats of strength and, more pertinently, the strongest men in the colliery. Cliff Jones, in all seriousness, mentioned the uncanny strength of Jac-Thomas-the-Lathe, who was busily working in the machine-shop next door. 'He can lift three men off the ground!' Cliff exclaimed. To be honest, Jac had never impressed me as a character of immense strength. In fact, he was a cheerful character, slightly lame, who had never demonstrated to me that he was extraordinarily strong.

'You see, boys,' Cliff expanded, 'since Jac has been handicapped in a certain way, nature has compensated him with supernatural strength in the shoulder and upper arm region.' All the boys without exception nodded in agreement.

'I doubt that,' I disagreed foolishly.

'All right, then, let's go next door and ask Jac,' said someone. Realising that I'd put my foot in it, I followed them into the machine-shop, to find Jac busily working his lathe.

At Cliff's request, he pulled the overhead lever to stop the lathe.

'Bill here does not believe that you can lift three men off the ground, Jac,' said Cliff.

Jac, with a broad smile on his genial face, lit up at the request.

'Sorry, boys, not today. I don't feel up to it.'

'Oh, come on, Jac, be a good sport! Don't disappoint the boy.'

With apparent reluctance, Jac took off his coat and rolled up his sleeves, to the delight of those present. He began to flex his muscles. Then, with slow deliberation, he bent his right arm and, flexing his muscles with the fingers of his left arm, he shouted, 'Biceps OK! Triceps OK!' He did the same exercise on his left arm. This was followed by a demonstration of knee-bends and bunny-hops, which amused those who were present. He breathed in deeply until his chest seemed twice the size. With the air of a circus performer, he tossed up various tools into the air and caught each one with a dexterity which won the admiration of his work-mates. During this process of warming up, the workshop had filled up with workmen from the colliery surface.

Jac, puffing slightly, asked for, 'Three volunteers, please.' There was a dash forward by many young men anxious to get into the act. 'Three, I wanted. Three of the same size. Thank you.' As he was speaking, he picked the ones he wanted and laid them on the floor, near and alongside each other. When I saw them on the floor I was more convinced than ever that Jac would fail in his attempt to lift the three. However, there was something strange about the whole affair and I remember feeling at the time that I was glad I was not involved in the charade. How could I have been so gullible?

'I haven't got the balance right yet,' said Jac, wrestling with the boy in the middle. 'He's too big.'

'What about Bill?' someone asked. 'He's about the right size.'

I could feel myself blushing at this unexpected attention. Jac looked at me as if he had seen me for the first time. He measured me with his eye from heel to head, and down again. He dashed forward like a ballet dancer to squeeze the muscles of my right arm and, with a knowing wink, pronounced, 'He'll do! Just the job! Perfect!'

There were sounds of approval as I, in a state of sheer embarrassment, made up the three in one of the outside positions. This pleased Jac and he reverted to a display of physical jerks and Indian dancing which caused merriment to all present. By this time he had built up a sweat and was ready to attempt his feat of lifting three men off the ground.

As he danced around, he suddenly decided to change the positions of the three, this time with me in the middle. It was then I realised that I had been tricked. Two heads rested on my upper arms and my forearms were held tightly by my two companions, whilst my outstretched legs were piniored down firmly by the legs of the other two. It dawned on me finally that something was amiss, and that I was going to be the main character of a great prank.

Jac by now was breathing fire, breaking the occasional wind and thundering his chest with his fists like Tarzan. The workmen rolled in laughter. Shouting at the top of his voice in Welsh, he would call, 'Pwy ddaw gyda fi i ymladd yn erbyn y Philistiaid?' – 'Who will come with me to fight against the Philistines?' – and in English 'Onward marched the six hundred, into the valley of Death'.

All at once he stopped. As he moved forward to attempt his feat the machine-shop was as quiet as a graveyard. With a screech, Jac moved forward and grasped the shirts of my companions as if in a frenzy. He jerked and pulled them, to no avail. Then he became silent and released his grip and began to laugh until the tears came to his eyes. My companions joined him, and so did everybody else. All except me.

The climax to Jac's performance had arrived. While I wrestled to get free, Jac opened the buttons of my trousers. I continued to struggle but I was held in a vice-like grip. My trousers were brought down to my knees, and my shirt lifted to show all my private parts to the workmen present. Someone produced a large oil-can and a bucket full of sawdust. Jac completed the ritual by squirting the oil over my abdomen, whilst another poured sawdust on the same area, for Jac to mix and rub, with somewhat apologetic glee, the mixture on to my genitalia, much to the delight of the assembled workmen.

I felt outraged and humiliated at the trick, but it was the initiation ceremony into the brotherhood of the colliery blacksmith's shop and I suppose I was right to accept the spirit of the baptism, as so many generations of boys had done before me. It was pointless trying to pinpoint the one person responsible, for they were all guilty in creating one big confidence-trick, Cliff and Jac being the principal actors.

I was to witness and take part in many of these ceremonies in the future – but I never expected to see it performed by players of the Cardiff Rugby Club in many of the bars at Oxford University when the club played there in 1953! The trick was the same, but the mixture was different; not engine oil and sawdust, but beer and sawdust. Many a scholarly undergraduate was caught by the old colliery trick.

By this time, at my parents' insistence, I attended night-school at the Mining and Technical Institute at Pontardawe, known affectionately throughout the Swansea Valley as the 'Tech', to follow its matriculation course. This move proved difficult: for three nights a week I had to catch a bus from the village at 4.45 p.m. and return at 10.45 p.m. with three hours' study in between. To be confined to this routine and the homework it entailed nearly drove me to despair.

However, I soon realised that there were many young men such as myself, keen on study in order to get out of the mines, who found night-school a pleasure. I made new friends. Their influence and personal ambitions awoke a desire in me to emulate their enthusiasm. In addition, there were really sympathetic and understanding teachers there, who encouraged their pupils all the while to do better things. Little did I know at that time that one day I would join the school as a member of its staff. What also proved helpful was the fact that many of the strikers in the blacksmith's shop were ambitious, and accordingly we used to exchange ideas and occasionally work out problems on the sides of coal-trams.

The blacksmith's workshop was an exciting place to work. Daily the blacksmiths toiled, making shapes out of iron and steel. They were grand to watch in their rolled-up flannel shirts, sweat dripping from their brows. The regular rhythm of their hammer on the anvil and the sight of the boy striker following the blacksmith's indications with harmonious understanding was a joy, despite the obvious hard work involved.

At this time I was playing soccer regularly for the village team, with an ex-Welsh League player, William John Hopkin, and a former goalkeeper, Danny Jones, putting me through my paces. I signed amateur forms for Cardiff City, which in itself was considered a big step forward, with William John and Danny encouraging me all the time. They were quite confident that I would be all right since the manager of the team, Cyril Spiers, had himself been a professional goalkeeper. They assumed, therefore, I would be tutored by him in the position. Much to my distress, he departed for Norwich AFC to become their manager before the new season had started. His successor was Billy McCandless, who brought with him, from Newport, a professional goalkeeper.

The Cardiff City of that period enjoyed a great following in south-east Wales, fielding three teams regularly on Saturday. I travelled twice a week to Cardiff to train, and in those days it was a long time to sit in various buses. There was no personal tuition, just practices, shooting goals, kick-abouts, pick-up sides; organised coaching had yet to be popularised. I played in some Welsh League games when one of the goalkeepers was injured. I remember speaking to Trevor Morris, the eventual secretary of the Football League of Wales, who was one of the administrative staff at the club at that time, concerning my prospects with Cardiff. He succinctly made my position very clear. 'The club possesses three professional goalkeepers who will commandeer the goalkeeping position because they will have to earn their keep. In the meantime, stay around. Watch the others. Improve your game. Your turn will come, Bill. After all, you *are* a reserve.'

Trevor had been sympathetic and I remained loyal to his advice until Christmas. Thereafter I began to skip training sessions, which did not please Mr McCandless, but I had somehow lost my keen interest in the game. It could have been that the numerous conversations about rugby at the smithy were gradually bringing influence to bear on my preferences.

During those days of no coaching, advice was always forthcoming about referees, players, trainers, club constitution and international rugby. The function of each position was explained to me and I was surprised at the complexity of the game. Often I would venture to talk about my own game, but soon there would be an impatience to revert to talk about rugby.

Question: 'What is the full-back's true position?'
Answer: 'His true position is ninth forward; his main function is to save the energies of his forwards.'
Question: 'How many ways are there of scoring a try in rugby without carrying a ball over the line?'
Answer: 'Six.'
Question: 'Why should the wing three-quarter carry the ball with his outside hand when running for the corner?'
Answer: 'He will need the inside hand to hand off.'
Question: 'Why should a half-back, in particular, not carry the ball in one hand when linking up with players?'
Answer: 'Because he is showing to the opposition that he does not intend to pass it.'

And so it would go on, gems of advice revealed in the normal course of rugby discussions.

Much to my surprise, I found that I had subconsciously acquired a knowledge of the game. The day-to-day indoctrination had worked and, incredible as it may seem, I found that in certain aspects of the game (for example, in remembering results, venues and scorers) I was more reliable than most. This one piece of specialisation changed my life in that company; I was at last accepted into their circle.

J.H.'s missionary work in Craig-cefn-parc lost its zeal and the club's existence came to a halt with the advent of the war. But when the war ended some of the better players joined the Vardre Club, which was in Clydach, two miles away. So the formation of the Death-Ray Stars had not been in vain after all: rugby had gained a few converts.

Very little football was played in the valley during 1940–45, for everybody was engaged in one way or another with the war effort. Wave after wave of German bombers devastated the town of Swansea. German bombs were aimed at the Mond Nickel Works in Clydach and at the National Oil Refinery at Skewen, which were obvious prime targets. Some stray bombs found their way to Craig-cefn-parc, especially incendiary bombs, which lighted the village like huge candles. The mine was used by some as an air-raid shelter until the threat of bombing abated.

As soon as hostilities ceased, there was a great upsurge of interest in the revival of all the major games in the valley. Sports clothing was difficult to purchase because of the scarcity, and football boots were a rare possession. Many a player was grateful to an ex-serviceman for bringing home a pair of boots so that he could play.

With this renewed interest in games, the quest for likely young players began with great intensity. I was asked by a committee member of the Vardre, who worked in the blacksmith's shop, if I would like to play for them. I was bowled over at his offer.

'What, me?' I replied. 'I am utterly clueless about how to play the game.'

'Never mind that,' he said. 'Play in the second row, you are big enough, you can hide in there.'

My first game was against Abercrave, one of the strongest teams in the Swansea Valley. I cannot recall catching the ball in the lineout, but I do remember having sore ears from packing in the scrums. 'You should have used Vaseline,' someone said afterwards. I cannot have made an impression, for I was not asked to play again.

In the meantime, I received letters from Cardiff City FC asking me to continue training, but I was losing enthusiasm because of the travelling involved and because of missing night-school. I had made one friend in Cardiff, a young man by the name of Cyril Hicks, who joined me in later years at PE College, but already I had made more friends by playing rugby. My soccer friends were annoyed, for they felt sure that I had a better future in soccer than in rugby.

I was taken completely by surprise when Moelwyn Jones of the Trebanos RFC asked me to play for them. When I suggested tentatively that I would like to play at full-back, they unexpectedly agreed. My reason for selecting such a position was evident: the position needed a goalkeeper's ability for catching and kicking a ball. But I was to discover that there was much more to the position than that, and after my first game in the position I was dropped. I was so ignorant of the game I really did not know why and nobody bothered to tell me what was wrong with my play. Such knowledge is not freely available. Many can condemn; only a few can correct.

During the following week I received a message that I was reserve for the next Saturday – an away game against Pontardawe. Pontardawe had been, at one time, one of the best sides in Wales and were trying to recapture their lost lustre. Trebanos, on the other hand, were a District League side trying to gain higher status. I turned up to watch the game without my rugby kit and discovered, much to my sorrow, I was needed to play. The chairman was furious when he found I was without kit and gave me a thorough ticking-off, and it did not help matters when he discovered that they had no spare supply. Eventually he borrowed from the Pontardawe club a pair of oversized boots without studs, two pieces of string to use as laces and a pair of dirty black shorts with a waistline to fit a fat lady, which needed my best red tie to hold them up.

The game was, surprisingly, an even one. It had been assumed that Pontardawe would run away with it, but Trebanos had, in Ronnie Harries at outside-half, a wily campaigner who had played in the RAF and for Llanelli.

'Stand opposite the outside-half,' said Ronnie, 'and measure his kicks so that you can stand in the right place if he fails to find touch.'

He nursed me through the game in this way, anticipating every move and telling me what to do beforehand. Ronnie was the goal-kicker of the team, but on this occasion he had failed to turn kicks into goals. Trebanos were awarded a kick on halfway and much to my surprise Ronnie told me to kick it. I refused politely, telling him that I did not know how. This shocked him so much that he impatiently dug a hole and placed the ball in it. 'Kick it,' he said, 'and make sure it goes straight between the posts.' That was the only score of the match, and the first time for Trebanos to beat Pontardawe, so they said.

During the course of the next few weeks, Ronnie took me out to teach me the fundamental skills of rugby football. He was the only person I ever met who was actually prepared to adopt the role of coach and teach me, man to man, certain skills of the game.

I continued to work in the blacksmith's shop, but had become rather rebellious in my attitude towards it. One day I was sent to work with a blacksmith who had a reputation for working with iron at substandard temperature, which made it hard to strike, bringing blisters to the palms of the striker's hands. When he brought to the anvil a piece of red-hot instead of white-hot iron, I suggested to him that he should return it to the forge fire for proper heating.

'Who is the craftsman here, boy, you or me?' he asked in anger. I remained sitting on my box in defiance. Three times he brought the red metal to the anvil and I remained where I was, unmoved. Not to be outdone he took off his apron and said, 'All right then, smart Alec, I'll get the gaffers to sort you out,' and off he went, storming with fury.

'You're for it,' said Cliff, as the two gaffers came into sight. 'Put the iron in the fire again,' one of them said to the blacksmith. Once more the metal appeared on the face of the anvil; the colour had not changed, so I stayed where I was. The gaffers were men of few words. 'Go down to the boilers,' one ordered. I did not realise it then, but I was never to return to the blacksmith's shop.

The boilers were equivalent to working on a chain-gang. During the course of a shift, one man using a wheelbarrow would wheel fifteen tons of coal from a truck a distance of ten yards to a large heap of coal which stood in front of the boilers. It was from this heap that the stokers would shovel coal into the blazing fires. Every machine on the colliery surface received a supply of steam from those boilers. Consequently, an abundance of ready coal was of the utmost importance to keep things moving. I wheeled steadily during the rest of the day and went home at the end of the shift utterly exhausted.

The following morning I returned to the blacksmith's shop, to be told I was not needed. Pretending not to care, I went to the torture house and began filling, wheeling and tipping the wheelbarrow at a

47

steady pace – but a steady pace was not good enough. At midday the huge stock of coal had disappeared and the stokers were without coal. The main haulage engine, which brought the coal from underground, was heard to splutter because of the lack of steam. This brought the manager and the colliery agent charging to the source of the trouble and to the person responsible – me.

'Quicken your pace up, lad. The main haulage engine has not got enough steam,' he said urgently.

'I have been working non-stop this morning without a meal break,' I replied, still keeping at my unhurried pace.

In no time at all, half a dozen labourers arrived on the scene and worked like Chinese peasants to restore the pile of coal.

'I will have no time to deal with you today. See me in my office first thing on Monday,' were the manager's parting words to me. Since it was Friday, I had a weekend before me in which to stew, I thought grimly to myself.

I stood before him on the Monday, and he shoved my cards towards me with his pencil.

'Here, take these. You are finishing today,' he said gravely. That announcement shook me, but not to be outdone I said, 'You are not half the man your son is!'

'What do you know about my son?' he asked with surprise.

'At least he would have asked my side of the story before taking action.'

'Answer my question. How do you know my son?'

I recounted a rugby match in which his son and I had played in the same team. His son was a dental student and consequently a social class higher than myself, but we had one thing in common and that was rugby football. He then asked me how I had landed in the boilerhouse, and I told him my story.

'All right, then, I'll give you another chance, but if you contravene any regulations in future, you'll be sacked instantly.'

That was an early indication to me that rugby football was a freemasonry. If you played rugby, high and low thought it important.

I was given many tasks in the colliery, such as driving an engine or looking after underground turbines, but I never seemed to enjoy doing them because they were painfully boring. I used to read books to break the monotony, for I had a feeling that my destiny was not in coal mining. My final job was on the surface, tipping colliery waste and slag on to one of those familiar tips which were spread at one time all over South Wales. It was really great working in the open – come snow, wind, rain or sunshine, it did not matter, for every day was a happy day. I worked with Aldwyn, Elwyn and Lew, and collectively we were responsible for the whole process of waste-disposal. Lew was a Bevin boy whose university education had been halted by the war and who had been designated to work in the colliery to do his National Service. He had been weaned on rugby football, having played for his public school and university. His companionship proved to be stimulating and my own knowledge of rugby began to increase because of Lew's experience. Rugby became our favourite topic of conversation.

We got along splendidly until one day he dropped a bombshell. 'I have just had notification that I can finish working here next Friday so that I can return to university,' he said happily. I looked at him incredulously.

'Congratulations,' I said sheepishly, realising that I was to lose my learned rugby friend.

'You'd better come too,' he said to me in all seriousness. 'You're wasting your life here.'

'What, me?' I said in astonishment. 'I have no trade or schooling.'

'That's not the point. You can always come back to this job.'

Lew and I left together on the Friday. He had a purpose. I had yet to find mine.

Chapter Four

Infatuation with Rugby

The Vardre Rugby Club in Clydach in the Swansea Valley was the natural club for the Graig boys to join, because it was only two miles down the road. Many of them had divided loyalties, however, and were influenced to join Trebanos or Glais RFC, neighbouring clubs of the Vardre, by more persuasive committee members belonging to these clubs. However, the Vardre was one of the most cheerful clubs in the West Wales League, a league which consisted of over forty teams. They languished in the bottom group of the league when I played for them, but that did not detract from their success, because they constantly provided first-class teams with players, and Wales with two internationals at that period – Gwyn Evans, wing forward, who played for the great Cardiff club, and Horace Phillips, wing three-quarter, who played for Swansea.

Gwilym was another player of note, probably the most fervent rugby player the Vardre had, and the most fanatical I ever met. Rugby dominated his life; nothing else mattered to him. His passion for the game was such that his parents bought him a milk-round so that he could have plenty of time to practise rugby in the afternoon. He had discovered when he was in the grammar school that he could tackle and had become expert at the ferocious crash-tackle. His great forte was to knock out his opponents. To hear him recount in Rengozzi's café in Clydach after chapel on Sunday night how he accomplished his best tackles was to witness a performance worthy of the finest stage.

The back room of the café would be packed with eager young

men, all anxious to share the rugby camaraderie and to jostle Gwilym into relating some of the stories of his fearsome tackles. He would be somewhat subdued at first, starting off quietly on how he made his initial assessment of his opponent – his size, speed and skill. His attention to detail entranced his audience and they remained transfixed as he prepared the way to flatten his prey. His voice would begin to rise and gather momentum as he stalked his quarry, a famous Welsh international, and inflicted on him his ultimate bone-shattering tackle to knock the player senseless. Such was Gwilym's sense of drama that many a young man would gasp with relief at the end of his story. For him, a good game was counted in 'scalps', not in tries and goals.

One is often reminded by older brethren how their parents related the great fervour of evangelical spirit which Christians experienced in 1904 in Wales. Such a feeling existed for sport immediately after the 1939–45 war. There was a passion for rugby which was unquenchable. Some of the small village clubs had a huge following. One cup-tie had over seven thousand people standing around the touchline.

One of the best-supported clubs in the West Wales League at that time was Amman United. The club organised four special trains to take their supporters to Llanelli's Stradey Park for a cup match against Felinfoel. When they played Cwmllynfell away in a cup match, seventeen double-deckers lined the streets in Garnant to take their lively and spirited fans to the match.

The Palais de Danse, 'Y Rinc', at Pontardawe was the meeting place for all the young people from the surrounding villages. It was there one rubbed shoulders with the great rugby stars of the area. They were adulated as superstars. It was considered a great honour to speak to them. I was gradually accepted as a member of the exclusive rugby fraternity. 'You've packed up soccer, then?' many would ask. It was at that period I realised that I had finally made the choice.

After playing rugby regularly for the Vardre for three months I made my first major rugby mistake. Swansea asked me to play full-back for them against Rosslyn Park. No one bothered to stop me, or to advise me not to play. Because of inexperience I played, and for that game I got away with it. The newspapers deemed me promising.

The following Saturday I was picked to play against another English club, Blackheath. Swansea had a near international on one wing, and Blackheath had, in Martin Turner, probably one of England's best post-war wings to play opposite him. Martin scored three tries that afternoon and since I was the last line of defence I was apportioned a share of the blame and deemed not so promising. However, a few months later, much to my amazement, Swansea's regular full-back confessed to me that he had feigned illness for the Blackheath game because he had played against the English winger during the war in the Middle East when Martin had run rings around him.

In education it is claimed that the best way of learning is by experience. My concept of rugby began to broaden as I played more frequently. I was certainly learning by experience as my circle of friends increased. One friend in particular was not only a very promising rugby player but also a splendid sprinter with ambitions to run for Wales. Unfortunately, he sustained an injury playing rugby which at first he, and his very anxious parents, thought not to be serious. They were mistaken; an operation was needed.

During his period of convalescence I remember him coming to the Graig in early autumn when the picturesque valley was in its most colourful splendour.

'Do you know, Bill,' he said, 'if I had my life over again I would not have played rugby.'

'Why is that?' I asked.

'It seems to me that players are only seeking fame, whether it be local, national or international,' he said, despondently.

'Come off it!' I said. 'You're a bit down on your health now; you'll soon change your mind when you get well again.'

Not to be outdone, he poignantly replied, 'Look at Banc-yr-Allt mountain and how beautiful it is. We hardly notice what is around us.'

I realised that the conversation had become depressing and quickly changed the topic for something more cheerful. Some time later he returned to the Swansea hospital, and such was our innocence we used to visit him on the way to rugby training at St Helen's, thinking we were cheering him up. We did not realise that our robust health and lively spirits distressed him until, one night, we were guided from the ward to an ante-room, where his tearful mother told us the bad news that there was no hope for our young sporting hero and that our presence in such large numbers upset him. We left the hospital in stunned silence because the revelation was, as far as we were concerned, completely unexpected. He died just before Christmas. His poignant words remain: '. . . seeking fame, whether it be local, national or international.'

Whilst the Vardre Rugby Club contentedly played rugby in the true spirit of the game with a 'win some, lose some' attitude, there were other clubs who were extraordinarily keen on winning. To win the West Wales League Championship or the West Wales Cup was for them the pinnacle of achievement. Certain clubs would go to great lengths to improve their teams in order to progress into the finals. There were, in that period immediately after the war, some unscrupulous committee men who would not hesitate to use unfair means in order to gain prestige and achieve success.

One such club was always in the forefront and inevitably appeared regularly in the final rounds of both competitions. When it was announced that their star full-back had become professional, by signing for a rugby league club, the news was such a shock to one or two of the committee members that it seemed the end of the world had come.

I came home from Sunday School to find a car outside our house, a very unusual occurrence in those days. When I entered the house my mother informed me that there were two gentlemen in the sitting-room who wanted to speak to me. They introduced themselves as the chairman and secretary of a particular club, one of the foremost pot-hunting clubs in West Wales, as it happened. They reminded me that their club had been, and intended to remain, one of the superior teams in the league despite their recent loss when their star full-back had joined a rugby league side.

'We are looking for a replacement for him. Would you be interested in joining us?' asked the chairman, in all seriousness. His proposition amused me, because it meant I would have to travel twenty-five miles across two valleys in order to play a *home* game. When I informed them of this, they had obviously pre-arranged an answer.

'We have considered that possibility and we are prepared to provide you with a taxi, and thirty shillings for every game you play.'

Clearly, I was being asked to be a professional in an amateur game, which was an embarrassing situation to be in at the time. The offer was a quarter of my wages and although I thought it was extremely generous, albeit rather amusing – for money was a taboo subject in rugby union – I discreetly rejected their kind offer. It shows how determined some clubs were to remain top in the West Wales League. The prospect of intruding on the privacy of a Sunday afternoon, which was sacrosanct at that time, did not stop them from turning every stone to keep their position in the two competitions, such was the importance of winning.

They say that lightning does not strike twice, but a similar offer occurred some years later when an unfashionable West Wales League club suddenly emerged in the pot-hunting game when they included three former Welsh internationals in their side. I was also approached by them with an even more attractive offer than before: thirty shillings, home and away, a meal and half a ton of coal every month. The entrepreneurial vision of those West Walian colliers makes me smile even now; it seemed that they had outwitted the WRU by decades in adopting sponsorship as an incentive. It was the small village team's way of ensuring a share of the glory that went with winning a shield or a cup.

Each club seemed to possess a character. The Vardre's was old Dan Jones, the treasurer of the club, who lived and breathed rugby football. He had no patience for any topic of conversation other than rugby. I remember him on one occasion stepping off the bus in Burry Port, over an hour late for the kick-off. He had spent most of the morning trying to get players and had been forced to use the bus to collect replacements from far and wide. The host chairman was rightfully indignant when the Vardre team arrived. 'We are going to report you to the League committee for arriving over an hour late for this match,' he blurted in anger.

'Report us to the League! Report us to the League!' replied Dan, equally angry. 'We have been halfway down to Carmarthen before we were told we had passed the village. There is no road sign to this outlandish place. I'll be the one to do any reporting! We've been on the road since one o'clock.' Dan's outburst seemed so genuine that the home chairman's anger abated, and he instantly changed his tune by apologising for his misunderstanding of the situation.

Dan did not care for any club but his own. The success of the Vardre was more important even than that of the Welsh team. 'They're up there; and we're down here,' Dan would say. Dan had a great respect for educated people, particularly those members of the clergy who could play rugby. One day he interrupted me as I entered the changing-room.

'I want you to do me a favour this afternoon.'

'Oh, yes,' I replied. 'What can I do for you?'

'We have a young curate playing for us today. A very good player who has played for the College of Lampeter. He is playing with you in the centre. Do me a favour, will you? Don't swear. We would like to keep him as a player.'

'I was not aware that I was swearing on the field, Dan,' I said with amusement.

'No, no, don't get me wrong. I am not accusing, Bil bach, but just a safeguard in case you should.' He hastened to add, 'We need another centre, see, and we don't want to upset him by using bad language, so don't swear, there's a good boy.'

Dear old Dan was the wisest of them all when it came to looking after the interests of the Vardre club. To Dan's generation it was an honour for the club to have a scholar in their midst.

No one complained when the curate arrived late, saying, 'Many apologies, chaps. Just put a dear old soul to rest, you know.' He spoke as if he'd been to Oxford, not Lampeter. He was dressed in black and as we changed we noticed that he had black-and-white football stockings underneath his trousers. 'Some curate,' we thought. During the course of the first half I found him very good at telling *me* how to play but not too expert at playing his own game, for a huge burly centre in the ranks of the opposition was finding a gap down the middle too often for my liking.

At half-time, our captain, who had worked a hard day at the coalface, suggested, with the wisdom of Solomon, that it would not be a bad idea if he attempted to tackle the centre in the second half.

'Don't worry, Skip, I'll bash him for six!' replied the curate with due grace and solemnity. The players, in the meantime, kept their heads low, as if to say 'wait and see'.

The game had restarted when the burly centre got the ball firmly in his hands and stampeded like a wild bull towards our new centre.

There is a correct and an incorrect way of tackling; our curate chose the latter and the tackle resulted in a collision which left him prostrate on the ground. I was the first by our reverend centre's side. When he recovered, his language was choice.

'Where is the dirty ***! Not fit to play the game!'

The players gathered round to see the damage to his Roman nose, which had turned sideways. His left cheek had been bruised and was visibly changing colour, and his left eye was already closed. He took no further part in that game and left the field, still swearing, much to the disillusionment of Dan Jones, who had come along to help.

I found that rugby was a great game when played in the true spirit of sportsmanship. Unfortunately, there are rugby players who do not enjoy themselves unless they injure or maim an opposite player. There was never a better sport than Dewi. He had given loyal and valuable service to his club, but he had become a nuisance. A nuisance in a nice way, so some thought; for Dewi was now thirty-nine years old but would persist in bringing his togs ('In case you are short, you see') for every home and away game. His regular presence upset one or two of the players and one expressed his thoughts in a most cruel way.

'Some buggers won't give in. If he played against me I would make sure to put the boot in.'

This remark offended one official, who quite indignantly retorted, 'You will never make the player Dewi was.'

Yes, indeed, Dewi had been a splendid player in his time. Strictly fair, he easily won the respect of the opposition with his gallant and spirited play. The evidence of his campaigns was written on his pale physical frame. One of his shoulder-blades showed an imbalance, for the tendons of his right shoulder had been ruptured in a long-forgotten game. There was an emptiness in his mouth when he smiled which bore testimony to the success of an opponent's deliberate blow. Dewi's ears were his trademark, an indication that he belonged to the game – not the boxing game, as some would insultingly suggest, but to rugby football, to which he was absolutely devoted. Dewi talked, breathed and dreamt rugby football; he could not give it up even though he was nearing forty years of age.

Committees too can be intolerant. The club was doing well, and there was no need for Dewi to carry his bag because there were reserves anxious to fill any gaps, should they occur. When a committee member one day cuttingly commented on his persistence, he withdrew to a quiet corner of the dressing-room and was thoroughly miserable. One of the current players took his side by exclaiming that Dewi had been a better player than any of the committee members, and this unexpected support made Dewi happy once again.

One Saturday Dewi's perseverance paid off; he was given the chance to play once more the game which was the lifeblood of his soul – not for his own club, but for the visiting team, who were one short! Little did he know he would never play again after that match.

'I was enjoying the game and was playing well until I was at the bottom of a ruck and then I had a kick in my back. It hurt something terrible, but somehow I managed to hang on until half-time. I dashed to the hedgerow to relieve myself, and I saw I was passing blood. I was frightened and I could feel the sweat come all over me. I played in the second half but it was hell. The end could not come quickly enough; when it did, I remember getting into the dressing-room, and no more.'

Dewi was propped up in hospital when he cheerfully recounted his last game. He had been taken home by car after his injury.

'There is no need for an ambulance, or a hospital, boys,' he had said. 'Just drop me off at the bottom of the road, not to upset the wife and kids, see.' Brave and guilty words, as one would expect from such a person as Dewi. It was his way of putting on a good face, not to worry those close to him and the ones he loved best.

'Stop the car here now, boys. I don't want the wife and neighbours to see me injured. I'll walk the rest of the way.'

His lion-heart was no good to him when he collapsed outside his council-house door with not one of his rugby friends there to give him a helping hand. His startled wife found him in a heap on the doorstep. Then came the trauma of the doctor's arrival, the ambulance and a panic-laden journey to the hospital.

'They have removed one of my kidneys and I feel fine,' said Dewi with a forced smile as he lay there in his hospital bed, the pain evident in his eyes. 'Looking forward to going home to the wife and kids, and back to work and to see some rugby.'

Dewi's ambition was only partly realised. He went home in due course but he never saw his work or a game of rugby again. He died at the end of three months.

The Llanelli Rugby Club is one of the foremost rugby clubs in Wales. It has a traditional infectious enthusiasm for the game which is unique, because most of it is expressed in the Welsh language. My joy was therefore unbounded when I was asked to help them out as a full-back on a pre-season campaign of missionary games against local second-class clubs. These games were never walkovers, but they were considered vital in fostering harmonious relationships with the junior clubs.

After playing in the first of these missionary games I had my first experience of being in the presence of a representative of the Welsh Rugby Union. It was after the dinner at the post-match function that he was called to speak by the chairman of the club.

'We have here tonight the WRU member, whom I have asked to speak to you.'

'Mr Chairman, secretary, treasurer, committee, honoured guests and players. It gives me great pleasure to come here tonight to pay tribute to this club and its officials. This club has officials who are hardworking, dedicated and envied by other clubs. The secretary is a brilliant organiser, the treasurer should be a banker, and the chairman is a visionary with great powers of leadership.'

His last remark concerning the chairman was rather strange, I thought, because the few words the chairman had spoken had been mumbled. 'I am glad to be here tonight,' he continued, 'to watch the Scarlets play against probably the best second-class club in Wales. This club is outstanding. Look at their enterprise in bringing the great Llanelli club here this evening. It was my duty to come here tonight as the member of the WRU for this area, but it is not a duty, but a pleasure. Thank you for inviting me. You know my telephone number if you want my help.'

All of us were impressed with the representative's speech. His patronising of the junior club had impressed me and I was convinced of his sincerity.

But that impression was dispelled, for in our next two missionary games the same local WRU member was in attendance, and when called upon to speak he gave exactly the same speech as he had done previously, much to the amusement of the Llanelli party. The only differences were the name of the club and the names of the officials, but the applause for him was equally resounding. I was beginning to understand the structure of the WRU and the various facets which belonged to it.

My performance at full-back for Llanelli must have impressed them, for I was sent a postcard informing me that I had been selected to play at home the following Saturday against Bath. Although I was thrilled with the selection, I was nervous at the thought of playing. When I got to Stradey, Llanelli's ground, I was met by the club's popular secretary, Mr Sid Williams, who informed me that my selection had been a mistake and that Ron Manfield from Pontypool had been transferred to the club and was already at the ground to play at full-back that afternoon. I did not object and thanked him for the three missionary games I had already played for the club; I was grateful for all small gestures. As it transpired, I had to play anyway, for Ray Williams (Llanelli, St Luke's and Wales), who was then doing National Service, had his leave cancelled and I was asked to play instead of him on the wing. Such was my naivety and lack of knowledge of the game of rugby, I agreed reluctantly, on condition that the centre did not bring me into the game.

The following Saturday I was selected as a reserve for the away game against Bristol. This, I came to understand later, was not a genuine selection but a gesture, on Sid Williams's suggestion, that I should be rewarded for being such a good sport, rather than being a good player, for it seems that Sid was impressed with my attendance record and my accepting Ron Manfield so graciously. According to Sid, 'Give him a trip to Bristol as a reward, and then forget him.'

Ray Williams (Llanelli and Wales) was supposed to have jumped on the train at Cardiff, but for some unknown reason he did not appear.

'Don't mind playing on the wing again for us today, Billy?' said Sid. 'I'll arrange for you not to get a pass.'

'Well, if you are short, Sid, I suppose I'll have to,' I said, without much confidence.

When the train had passed through the Severn tunnel, the players began to talk about the impending game. It was revealed that the opposition's biggest threat would be an English wing three-quarter and, as the captain Ossie Williams said, 'It's up to you, Bill, to keep him quiet.'

With this bit of information, I instantly cornered Llanelli's other wing and asked him to change sides with me. I had no solace from him. 'I'm not going to risk my reputation against that chap.'

I found myself on the field marking one of the two best wings in England. I was on edge, and when Bristol passed the ball along the three-quarters with the intention of getting it to their star wing, I dashed up in a panic, like a greyhound set loose from a trap, to receive a pass intended for the Bristol wing, and I ran some thirty yards to score a try under the posts. When I walked back, I sensed a new mark of respect for me as a player, and when the captain, Ossie, said, 'Move the ball to the wings, boys,' I felt aglow.

After the Bristol match I became a regular Llanelli player at wing three-quarter, although I had a feeling that I could make a better full-back. Once one made the grade, things began to happen. I became the recipient of those brown sealed envelopes (containing a pound note and a few shillings and pence) discreetly handed out by the honorary treasurer 'to cover the cost of bus fares to the ground for training sessions or matches'. This happened right under the nose of a WRU executive member who, it seemed, had conveniently forgotten that it was against the rules for players to receive any remuneration. Or was he afraid that if he rocked the boat he would lose the club's vote in the next election?

The club's 'brown envelope philosophy' was fully justified. It ensured that each player had more than enough cash after the match not only to buy beer for himself but also to purchase a pint or two for his counterpart in the ranks of the opposition. You could buy sixteen pints of beer for a pound in those days.

Other clubs, I discovered, operated a sliding-scale system whereby the prima donnas received a bountiful pay-out and the second-fiddlers the merest trifle. At Cardiff, where home games sometimes attracted as many as forty thousand spectators, the visiting club's entourage as well as their own would be supplied with a cask or two of Brain's beer and could drink themselves blotto if they felt like it.

The tough West Wales clubs were a law unto themselves, especially if they had a chance of winning the League and Cup. The chairman of one of them, a family butcher, supplied sweeteners in the shape of legs of lamb or pork to attract star players; another chairman, a county councillor, would ensure that players found employment as teachers or in the police force. Strict adherence to the amateur code was a matter of interpretation: the pragmatist proclaimed 'God loves winners'; the Corinthian responded with 'Thou shalt not cheat'.

That one appearance in Bristol triggered off the most unexpected of requests. The following week I had a letter from one of the prominent clubs in the West Country of England, asking me if I was prepared to play for them regularly. 'If you like it down here, there is a job ready for you. Could you drop me a card at once, whatever the verdict?'

This practice by the West Country clubs was not uncommon before the last war, because many a Welshman gifted in rugby was tempted to leave Wales in order to get a decent living in England, and rugby was a passport to achieving this. It seemed that, after the hostilities of war, some people attached to rugby clubs in England were still practising the pre-war job-incentive rugby schemes in Wales.

A few months later, two of us were invited to spend a fortnight playing rugby in Cornwall at Easter time, all expenses paid. The club had an overcrowded fixture list with some top teams on tour, and they wanted to augment their playing strength with some Welshmen, who, they took for granted, could play really well. We accepted the invitation and played in seven matches, thoroughly enjoying ourselves in the process. We were offered job opportunities which we turned down, much to the disappointment of our hosts.

Chapter Five

Rugby League or College Rugby?

It was not only clubs in the West Country who were anxious to procure the services of Welsh players, but the more sinister rugby league clubs of the north of England. Although there was a distinct feeling against rugby league in Welsh rugby union circles, there was at that time a measure of good feeling and sympathy towards those players who elected to become professionals by crossing Offa's Dyke, never again to play in their homeland as amateurs.

Llanelli's headquarters at the time was the Salutation Hotel. It was quite an experience, therefore, to be accosted in the toilet of the hotel by rugby league scouts. 'Would you like to play for Batley or Huddersfield?' I even had a letter sent to my home: 'Meet me at the Grand Hotel, Swansea, where we can discuss arrangements.'

Rugby league belonged to our folklore. It was part of our rugby history. No one would have a strong objection to a local player going north. There was no malice, but a feeling of support: 'If he can improve himself, the best of luck to him.' But the supporters would remain steadfast in their allegiance to the amateur code. Nowadays there is no need for a Welsh rugby star to go north to play for money. Neil Jenkins, the Pontypridd superstar, recently contracted himself to his club for five years for a sum in the region of £1 million. Even before such huge amounts of money were available, the inducements to remain were so tremendous – journalism, TV and radio, businesses, etc. – that the exodus of migrating rugby talent practically ceased.

It was not so during the time of Bilo Rees, who went north in 1921. He was from the village of Garnant in the Amman Valley and played for Amman United, a powerful second-class team of that period. Llanelli spotted his brilliance, Bilo was invited to join the famous club and he became an instant star, certain to play for Wales. He worked in a local pit producing the tough anthracite coal which at the time was abundant in the valley. When he returned home from work one day, his mother told him of the two visitors from England who had called to see him. She did not fully comprehend what they wanted, but it had been made clear to her that they would wait for him at the Half Moon Hotel in the village. Mrs Rees's language was Welsh, and English was foreign to her.

When Bilo received this information, he bathed and, full of curiosity, went to meet the two mysterious English gentlemen. When he returned, later on in the afternoon, he was in a dazed mood. His mother was anxious to discover the purpose of the strange gentlemen's visit.

'Sit down there, Mam,' said Bilo, pointing to a chair which was near the kitchen table, while he himself did the same.

'What did those men want, Bilo?' she asked nervously. 'You are not in some kind of trouble are you?'

Bilo smiled at her concern. 'No, Mam,' he said. 'They are gentlemen from the north of England, and I have signed to join the Swinton Rugby League Club.'

Mrs Rees was not quite sure of the affairs of rugby football. 'What is wrong with Llanelli then? I thought you were happy with them.'

'Llanelli will never want me to play for them again when they hear the news.'

'What news? You've done no wrong.'

Bilo then explained to her that he was going to play professional rugby in the north of England and that he would be leaving Garnant for good on the following day. A job was waiting for him and from that moment onwards he would be paid for playing rugby. As Bilo was speaking to his mother, his hand went into his coat pocket and produced a thick envelope.

'You have been good to me, Mam, and I want you to take this money to help you and the rest of the family.'

Bilo had opened the envelope and placed £500 in white five-pound notes on the table. His poor mother, with mouth agape, burst into tears.

'Bilo bach! Bilo bach! They have deceived you. That is not money.' The dear lady had never in her lifetime seen a white five-pound note before.

Bilo became a legend in the league game. He appeared in eleven Tests for Great Britain (1926–29) and toured Australia in 1928, making more appearances than any other player. He appeared in six rugby league internationals for Wales. Swinton were a major force in Bilo's days, winning the Rugby League Cup, Championship, Lancashire Cup and League in the season 1927–28, and they were the third and last team to perform this feat. Bilo played in four Challenge Cups and won two, in 1926 and 1928; four Championships and won two; and won four Lancashire Cup finals. He was a natural Welsh half-back who could play with equal felicity at either inside- or outside-half.

Such was Bilo's fame and popularity, I remember his fans coming from far and wide to speak to him at the Colliers Arms, Clydach, where he was landlord, long after he had retired. He was a happy, bubbling enthusiast for life, with a ready-made fund of reminiscences about rugby league in all corners of the globe. He had an infectious smile which conveyed a warmth of greeting from his small stature. His greatness in rugby football can be measured from the fact that his name is included in the *Encyclopaedia Britannica* as one of the greatest sporting innovators ever to have played the game and certainly as one who helped rugby league to achieve popularity.

When Independent Television first broadcast its Welsh-language programmes, they were transmitted from a studio in Manchester in the afternoon, not only to Wales but to the rest of the UK as well. Any Welsh TV producer worth his salt would inevitably have included Bilo on one of his TV programmes and, when he did appear, no one ever thought of the repercussions. It caused a sensation. Bilo had finished playing league rugby thirty years previously but when his face appeared on the screen, speaking in a foreign language, it caused a great stir in Lancashire and Yorkshire. The little Welsh grasshopper who had given them such pleasure and happiness was on TV, alive and well. When the programme finished, the telephone did not stop ringing for days, such was his popularity.

I never saw him play, but I can vouch for his modesty and humility. He was always lavish in his praise of others but never of himself. Perhaps this can be portrayed by an example. A famous journalist who knew nothing about rugby league football wanted, if possible, a former Welsh rugby league star to join him, all expenses paid, at a rugby league cup final at Wembley. As it happened, one of Bilo's friends, Evan Glyn Hopkins, came to know of the request and immediately got in touch with the journalist and told him he had found a former star with expert knowledge of the game.

It transpired that both Evan and Bilo were invited and, indeed, thoroughly enjoyed the grand occasion. When the game had finished, Bilo wanted, in his own way, to repay the journalist for the fine time they were having. He decided to take them to the hotel where a celebration dinner for both teams was to take place. Bilo was sure there would be a reception for him and his friends in the lounge bar. They would wait hopefully for someone whom Bilo knew to pass by.

A group of well-groomed gentlemen alighted from a taxi and walked in their direction, oblivious, it seemed, to their presence. All at once Bilo stiffened and stood to attention, taking off his cap at the same time. 'How are you, sir?' he asked in his soft, modulated voice. The leader of the group stopped in his tracks and then, in instant recognition, enveloped Bilo in his arms, clapping him on his back and pumping his hand with great delight whilst his companions were anxiously awaiting their turn to share in the act.

Bilo and his two friends were fêted like kings that night in the company of Bill Fallowfield, the former secretary of the Rugby League, and his committee. When it was time to leave the festivities, Mr Fallowfield accompanied them to the main door and his final words to Bilo were, 'Don't you ever raise your cap to me again, Bilo. I am the one who should be raising it to you.'

No wonder Bilo became a legend, but he was not the only Garnant product to make the grade. David Davies, popularly known locally as 'Dai Cender', also came from the village of Garnant. I met him when he worked in the same colliery as I. His brother, Jac, was also a league player, having played for Dewsbury. Both were very impressive personalities.

Dai, now eighty, had wanted to go north as others in the valley dreamed of becoming preachers and teachers. 'I wanted to play rugby league. It was my ambition.' You could see the mischief, the guile, the resolution of a scrum-half in his whole being without asking him what position he played. He gesticulated and demonstrated his actions during the course of a conversation which indicated quite clearly that he must have been an extraordinarily gifted scrum-half. His local teams were Amman United and Neath. 'I used to get more money playing down here than I did up north in my first season,' he said, with a wicked wink.

Dai was twenty-two when he joined Broughton Rovers in 1925. 'I was earning a pittance in the pit for working hard in difficult and dangerous conditions. How could I refuse money for playing in the fresh air? We were a big family, six boys and two girls. It was a heaven-sent opportunity for me.'

He fancied Broughton Rovers because the famous James brothers of Swansea had played for them at half-back. Dai could hardly speak English when he got to Manchester, but he took to the game like a duck to water. Much to his dismay he found that Broughton were not a very good team, and because they were not winning, the wages of the players were very low. This did not suit Dai and he became one of the agitators to improve things. During a players' meeting, an ex-army officer and the chairman of the club – a General, Dai called him – began laying down the law.

'Now then, Davies,' said the General.

'Hold the boat a minute, now,' said Dai. 'You call me Dai or Mr Davies, for I've got a handle to my name, if you please. You may have been a General on the field in the Somme, but I am the General on the rugby field, as far as this club is concerned.'

It seemed that Dai's directness upset the board and, since Dai by this time was fed up with the club, he asked for a transfer. This was a bombshell because Dai was the most popular and talented player the club had and there were howls of protest from the fans. 'Broughton star for transfer' was the headline on the back pages of the northern papers. Among the clubs interested in Dai were Warrington, Wigan – who had the great Welshman Jim Sullivan playing for them – and Oldham.

Oldham was the club that Dai fancied most. As a subtle inducement, they were prepared to offer him a magnificent pub outside the gates of the Oldham ground. This would have given Dai the chance to bring his parents from Wales to serve behind the bar and also bring the children with them. But Dai's good intentions fell by the wayside, for whereas he thought nothing of leaving Wales, his parents did not relish the idea of adapting themselves to live in a new and, to them, foreign environment.

Evan Phillips, also from Garnant, a team member of Broughton, told a member of the Warrington board that Dai was signing for Oldham that night. It was not true, but it inflated Dai's value to a £1,000 transfer fee, a big sum in those days. In addition to that fee, two players were given as well, and Dai received £250 (an undisclosed part of the transaction).

Dai revelled in the life. He loved playing; sometimes life was rough, but living with the northerners was honey and roses to him. 'When you played well they loved you, and since I was a Jack-in-the-box type of player I was usually in their good books.'

Dai had the dubious distinction of having played in four rugby league cup finals and lost on each occasion.

'I shook hands with the Prince of Wales in the first ever cup final to be played at Wembley. What I thought was a good omen went sour for me, for Warrington lost by seventeen points against Huddersfield. I scored two tries, but they were not enough.'

David Davies enjoyed his stage, the rugby league grounds of Lancashire and Yorkshire. He must have delighted hundreds of thousands of people with his skill and audacity. One could see the devil in him as he demonstrated his flick-passes with an imaginary ball.

'I postponed my wedding three times in order to play in the trials to pick the best to go to Australia. They went without me. Three trials, that was a bitter pill to swallow. Fancy going to Australia! I would have shown them. But the supporters knew my worth and made a banquet for me and the missus to ease us of our disappointment. Best hotel in the town. Look at that grand clock over there with the inscription on it. That's what they gave me.'

It had pride of place on the Welsh dresser and one could see the sadness of it all: on the losing side in four rugby league cup finals, to appear in three trials to select the Great Britain side to Australia and not make it after all.

Surely the game must have soured Dai? Not a bit of it. 'I was offered the best pubs in Warrington, but Mam could not stand the smell of them at the time. Mind you, we have kept a few since.'

'Would you tread the same ground again, Mr Davies?' I asked finally.

'Yes! Oh yes! Sooner than last time. It's a grand game. Suited my nature, see. You can see I am a bit of a fox.'

Others went up north from the Amman Valley. Emrys Evans from Cwmgors was capped for Wales as prop and wing forward before he went north. A post-war star, again from Garnant, was Ted Ward, who at one time held the record number of points scored in one season. Ted was an exceptional player, a superstar, who toured Australia and captained Wales on nine occasions.

In the immediate post-war period rugby league scouts were everywhere. I was tempted to go north to Halifax by their secretary, Bill Hughes, a schoolmaster who hailed originally from Ystalyfera in the Swansea Valley. Two of Halifax's directors came to Craig-cefn-parc on a Sunday afternoon when I was, again, in Sunday School. When I met them I found them to be warm-hearted, businesslike and strictly above board. I did not sign because I had something going for me in the pipeline; but if that failed, I would immediately get in touch.

It was Ray Williams, the Llanelli wing three-quarter at the time, who provided me with the incentive I wanted to hear: 'St Luke's College will want a full-back next season, you can fill the bill. Why don't you apply so that you can qualify as a sports master?' I could probably have accomplished my teacher's training in the north and played rugby league, but the lure of going to the famous St Luke's was far more important to me at the time. Ray's encouragement did the trick; I followed his advice and was, in due course, accepted.

When I started teaching I found it strange that my connection with Halifax was recurring. When I look back at my teaching career, many boys stand out as being extraordinary in one way or another, but one boy was like a beacon. Welsh rugby fans are all familiar with the legendary Bob Scott, the superb New Zealand full-back of the '50s who used to practise kicking goals with his bare feet. A boy, Ron James, aged fifteen, used to make me wince when he used to accomplish the same feat from halfway, bare-footed, with the old-fashioned leather rugby ball with laces, and, with faultless consistency, rain or shine, put it over the posts. Ron was one of the best prospects I had ever seen and it was not a surprise to me to discover later that he had a final trial for Wales when playing for Maesteg. He joined Halifax at a very young age and gave the club glorious service.

St Luke's had accepted me with the provision, so the captain of the rugby club had said, that I improved my ability to play full-back. With this object in mind I did not turn up in the Llanelli trials to retain my position as wing three-quarter, but instead joined Glais in the West Wales League in order to improve my knowledge of full-back play. On reflection, it was a silly thing to do, but advice in those days was not freely available. However, I enjoyed playing with Glais and the experience improved my game.

The following Christmas, Llanelli asked me to reconsider playing on the wing for them, but I foolishly refused their kind offer, saying that full-back was my position now.

St Luke's College, Exeter, was a small college in comparison with today's colleges of education. There were just over three hundred male students there in 1950, most of them ex-servicemen anxious to be trained as teachers. The St Luke's Rugby Club was the sixth oldest club in England, formed in 1860. There was a period when rugby was deemed to be unfitting for the development of boys, and it was thought wrong for student-teachers to be encouraged in the barbaric game. Accordingly there was a forced cessation of play there – but that philosophy did not prevail for long.

In Mr James Smeall, MA, the principal, a former London Scottish loose forward, the college had a gifted man, exceedingly keen on rugby football. He was devoted to the attainment of excellence in all aspects of education and possessed a profound respect for all talents. For those who set a bad example, or those who did not try their best, he was a hard man. His love of rugby was unrivalled. It was claimed that he had a special drawer in his desk which contained a special, and separate, list of applications from candidates with superlative rugby pedigrees. To counteract that bias towards rugby, it was also claimed he had another drawer which contained a separate list of candidates with exceptional brains, to balance those whose talents were more evident on the rugby field.

Whatever was the mystery behind Mr Smeall's philosophy? There is abundant evidence that his vision of rugby as a game well worth playing has borne universal fruition. The long list of ex-students who have graced international rugby is praise enough – but to have produced many fine rugby teachers and dispersed them to the four corners of the globe to spread the cause of rugby has been a major contribution towards the universal popularity of the game.

The influx of Welsh players to the college was attributed to Horace Edwards, Llandovery College, Neath and former Welsh final trialist. Horace was a superlative centre who had been chosen to play for Wales against Ireland but unfortunately was denied the opportunity because of snow. Mr Smeall had been impressed with Horace's play when he had watched Neath play at Exeter. It is not known whether it was deliberate or accidental that they met at the bar of the hotel later that evening, whereupon Mr Smeall complimented Horace on his scintillating play. Praise about his rugby skill was not uncommon to Horace. However, they chatted. In the course of their conversation Mr Smeall discovered Horace's educational qualifications. They were good enough to offer Horace a place at St Luke's to study PE. The surprising offer came out of the blue as far as Horace was concerned, and he was delighted. It was an offer he could not refuse, and, better still, the offer was open to his rugby friends, as long as they could meet the educational requirements.

The gate was opened which enabled hundreds of brilliant young rugby players to go to St Luke's to train as teachers. The tradition lasted until the late '70s when an invisible power absorbed the college into Exeter University, thus burying the name St Luke's for ever. At Easter time in 1982, Exeter University failed to fulfil its fixtures in South Wales. It could not raise a team. At the same time three former St Luke's players were conspicuous in the home championship: Slemen and Scott (England) and Squire (Wales).

Exeter's outlandish location in those days proved to be a blessing to the development of rugby football at the college. The fixture list contained a mixture of second- and first-class teams, which was ideal opposition for the young players. Whenever the college played at home, crowds used to gather around the touchline with the principal and Mrs Smeall the staunchest of supporters. He used to be very keen on standards.

It happened one day that I was walking on to the field to play in a match, when Mr Smeall, walking from a group of spectators, came and spoke to me quietly.

'Mr Samuel,' he said, 'surely you are not going to play in those dirty boots?' I could feel myself flushing the colour of beetroot. 'Go back to your room, old chap, and clean them. They can play without you for a while.'

Not only did he regard the rugby pitch as being sacred, he also considered the daily morning service an essential part of the college's routine. He would be there without fail. I happened to miss a service one morning and, during the afternoon, I was walking through the glorious gardens of the college when I met Mr and Mrs Smeall.

'Good afternoon, Mr Samuel. Are you better?' asked Mr Smeall.

'I was not aware I'd been ill, sir,' I replied.

'Thank heavens for that! I missed you in chapel this morning, and I was telling my wife that you must be ill,' he smiled. I had no reply to that. I attended every service possible thereafter and made sure to apologise for any absences in future.

There had been an enthusiasm for rugby at the colliery, but rugby in St Luke's was a frenzied fanaticism. It was the whole day's topic of conversation. Young men with unbounded talent for the game practised, experimented and discussed tactics and fitness-preparation schemes. They were keen, perceptive and hungry to gain as much rugby knowledge as possible. St Luke's was the ideal place to satisfy all their rugby ambitions.

I believe that teachers are born rather than made and this was true in the case of Mr Eric Sparrow, the lecturer in charge of my group. He spoke in a broad Lancashire dialect – when he forgot himself. His lectures were thoughtful, purposeful and full of humour. He possessed a compassion for his fellow men. The clever would receive praise from Mr Sparrow, as would the non-gymnast, like me. My group idolised him, for he encouraged us to become good teachers by his own personal example.

His system of introducing us into the art of teaching was very simple. He would listen to one student teaching another student, then, progressively, one student to six, one student to twelve and, finally, one to thirty. If, by this time, the student could not teach, he would start once again.

At twenty-seven years of age, I was the odd man out in our PE group, for, because of my maturity, I could hardly do any gymnastics. My vertebrae had stiffened, probably from working in the colliery. My gymnastic shorts, which he had used in the tropics, had been given to me by an old sailor, while my gym shoes had been bought in Woolworths in Swansea. My fellow students were in modern gymnastic clothing. At that time I was not too keen on spending money to be like them.

However, Mr Sparrow had arranged for a class of thirty boys to come to the college gymnasium from one of the schools in the city so that the students could have some practice teaching them in real conditions. I remember being told by Mr Sparrow that I was to teach the boys a game at the end of the lesson. Since I had not taught before in front of an audience I was not looking forward to it, with some forty students and three lecturers on the stage; the students, in particular, were a fun-seeking lot and if I were to falter they would not hesitate in having a laugh at my expense.

The lesson went beautifully and when it came to my turn I could hear one or two of my mates having a laugh. I was determined to make a good showing and, unknown to them, I had been practising on my own. The game was a relay, 'running with determination with a rugby ball', and it went off perfectly.

'Well done!' said Mr Sparrow. Then, in a whisper, 'Give a demonstration. We've got time to spare.'

I turned to the class. 'Nearly right!' I exclaimed. 'But you are not determined enough. Watch me!'

At the other end of the gymnasium was a pair of swing doors which remained perfectly motionless.

'Tuck the ball firmly under your arm and really run flat out,' I shouted, and I ran as quickly as I could, past the waiting boys, whose eyes were fixed on me. I must have looked an idiotic figure, with the ball tucked underneath my arm. As I was getting to the end of the gymnasium, I slowed down and my Woolworth daps shot from under me, leaving me to slither on my back with my feet in the air through the swing doors, stopping in the corridor outside. There was I, all alone in the corridor, with the sound of the swing doors moving to and fro and, from inside, a crescendo of laughter from my fellow PE students, whom I had to face in the next few seconds.

When I pushed open the door it was worse than I expected. The ball was still under my arm and blood was trickling down from a burn on my thigh. The poor boys had not budged, and remained unsmiling despite the uproarious laughter of my colleagues. I thanked the boys for helping us with the lesson and dismissed them.

When we were left to our own devices we all had an extra laugh. Nearly thirty years later some former students reminded me of the 'swing-door incident'.

I remember too the athletics lessons we used to get from Mr Smith. He was a former Scottish champion in the shot putt and long jump, we were told. I could manage to throw the discus and shot and also, as a rugby player, cope with the running events. Mr Smith was anxious that we should be able to coach all aspects of athletics, including the pole-vault. I was curious about this event, but after seeing it being performed lost all interest at once.

'It's Mr Samuel's turn now!' said Mr Smith.

'After the next one, if you please, Mr Smith. I haven't got the hang of it yet.'

The next to go was a red-headed, bespectacled young Yorkshireman named Alan, who was a natural product of that lovely county ('There's nowt he can't do!'). His running with the pole was first-class, and so was his planting of the pole. When he got up to the vertical, however, he stayed there for a few seconds while the spectators scurried aside. Which way would he fall?

Gravity decided to bring the pole down against the upright stanchion with a bang. Poor Alan – his back was as red as his hair and he was in terrible pain, but he had plenty of spirit and was as right as rain in five minutes.

'Whose turn was it?' asked Mr Smith.

'Mr Samuel, sir!' was the reply.

It was then that Mr Smith and I had a difference of opinion. As a teacher, it would be wrong of him to finish the lesson on such a note; the boys, or students in our case, would suffer some apprehension concerning the event if he did not achieve success.

'Now then, Mr Samuel, get ready,' said Mr Smith.

'Sorry, sir, if God had intended me to pole-vault he would have provided me with a pair of wings,' I said conclusively. My remark caused great amusement, and the laughing Mr Smith called it a day.

The highlight of our rugby experience in St Luke's was a three-match tour of the south of France, when we were invited to play against the renowned first-class clubs of Tarbes, Oloron and Dax. We flew to Paris and travelled overnight to Tarbes, which was an experience in itself in those days. It was vastly different from the days when that great All-White player, Dai White, went with the Swansea RFC for a fortnight's rugby tour of France in the '30s and arrived at Swansea's High Street railway station with no luggage. 'Where is your luggage, Dai?' asked the secretary with alarm. Dai went to his pocket and produced a spare collar for his shirt. 'That's all I'll need, boys,' he replied with a smile.

It was our first experience of the carnival spirit of French rugby. Small matches preceded the featured match, while a market and a funfair were simultaneous attractions. The French promoter of the tour was a real live-wire, and a brilliant organiser. He declared at the beginning of our stay that when the tour was finished he intended to invite four St Luke's players to revisit the south of France to play as guest players for the University of Lyons in a special game he was promoting. This proved to be an incentive for all the players to be on their mettle. When, at the end of the tour, he announced the names of Harry Thomas, Llanelli RFC, the captain; Bryn Meredith, Wales and British Lions; Goronwy Morgan, Swansea and Coventry; and myself, there were typical shouts of 'Fixed!', 'Shame!' and 'Pets!'.

When we returned on the second visit, we were confronted with a surprising proposition. Our host was the most amenable of men, with a passion for rugby, French rugby in particular. It came as a bombshell to us when he calmly suggested that he wanted us to consider becoming full-time rugby coaches in the south of France. We were quite naturally taken aback by his offer, for it had never entered our heads that such jobs existed.

He saw that we were stunned by his words, but it did not dissuade him from continuing to endorse his offer. 'When you have finished in college, you will be trained teachers of physical culture with a know-ledge of rugby football and how to play it with magnificence. I will arrange for you to work in the summer as couriers for my travel agency, whilst in the winter you will be designated to play and coach a particular rugby club. At the end of three months you will be fluent in French. As for payment, it will be better than what you will earn as teachers.'

All this appeared to me, at the time, a well-rehearsed offer. We were certainly excited and tempted by his philanthropic idea, but when the analysis was over, 'Hen Wlad Fy Nhadau' seemed far more nostalgic away from home than it did at the Arms Park. With mixed feelings we declined his potentially wonderful offer. I wonder how Wales and the Lions would have managed without Bryn Meredith? What is interesting now, of course, is the fact that France were seeking ways and means of improving their national game eighteen years before Wales moved in that direction.

One of the finest things that happened to me at St Luke's was that I became conscious of being Welsh. There is a saying that a Welshman is a better Welshman after a period of being away from his native land. This I have found to be true. It was at Exeter that I discovered the anger and frustration of the East Walians at their inability to join in Welsh-language songs which the West Walians sang naturally. It was a ludicrous situation when Welsh students had to go to an English college to learn Welsh songs. In contemporary Wales, the question may be posed: is it right for the Local Education Authority and the parents to decide whether children should speak Welsh or not? Surely it is for the children to decide, for when they come of age they can decide for themselves whether to continue with it or not.

The East Walians at St Luke's never had that chance, but Welshness to them seemed far more important than it did to us. They were bitter and resentful of their inability to join in with the rest of us. However, the regular Welsh contingent that graced the famous college, Welsh-speaking or not, were eagerly desired there for their singing, sense of drama and ability to play rugby. They remained loyal to it until it disappeared into oblivion – another victim of bureaucracy.

Chapter Six

Branded Failures

At the end of my two years at Exeter I decided to move to the new PE college at Whitchurch in Cardiff, to pursue a diploma course in PE. My reasons seemed quite sensible at the time. A new staff would have new ideas. The move meant I would be nearer home and my girlfriend, Velda, whom I wisely married later on. The Cardiff Rugby Club was another incentive. It was considered to be one of the best rugby clubs in the world, at times drawing home crowds in excess of twenty thousand people. I wanted to experience the training methods the club used at that time and compare them with what we had learnt at Exeter.

The college complex at Cardiff was an old, dilapidated army camp dominated by a huge gymnasium, whereas St Luke's had been dominated by a chapel and buildings which were in the process of being restored from those showing wartime damage into attractive period buildings.

Never judge a book by its cover, as they say, for treasure can be found in the most unexpected of places. The teaching and philosophy of physical education at Whitchurch was of a very high order indeed. Both Mr Eric Thomas, Principal Lecturer, and Mr Gwyn Williams were of the old school, dedicated towards gently guiding one's thought to becoming a better teacher. Mr Sid Aaron was entirely different, a man of immense gymnastic skill who was completely intent on raising the gymnastic performances of all his students, and since I was not inclined that way, I had a hard time. No lesson with him was complete unless every available minute had been used and one would end up thoroughly soaked in perspiration.

He never relaxed. One of his greatest attributes was that he neglected no one. He would not place the gymnastic duffers, like me, in the corner and ignore them, as many teachers do, but instead, with great patience, made sure that we were physically educated too. Mr Aaron had a considerable influence on my teaching life. He was strict, fair and compassionate. Quite subconsciously, I managed in due course to model my approach to teaching on both him and Mr Sparrow, although they were different types of teacher.

On reflection, neither St Luke's nor the college at Cardiff had nominated members of staff to act as coaches to the rugby club. It was left to the captain and committee to adopt a policy for playing, and for the captain to implement it. It would be ridiculous to confine embryonic PE masters to the demands of a simple coaching certificate; their knowledge should be far in excess of that. When St Luke's scored over a thousand points in 1953, they did so without a coach being near the place.

There was plenty of enthusiasm for rugby at the college, but the standard in comparison with St Luke's at that time was inferior – as one would expect, for there were only a few students in the college. I had the good fortune of being elected captain – a step up for me: I had been vice-captain at St Luke's.

I realised a personal ambition by joining the world-famous Cardiff Rugby Club, who had so many players wanting to play in their ranks that they were the only club I was aware of that needed a trial to select a trial team to play against the Cardiff Second XV. From that trial, a team consisting of new faces and the Second XV would be selected to play in the final trial against the Cardiff First XV.

The club had a galaxy of stars, some of them equal to the superlatives used to describe them by over-zealous journalists, whereas there were others who were of quite ordinary ability. With half-backs of the calibre of Rex Willis and Cliff Morgan, the club had a springboard to enterprising, free-flowing rugby. Bleddyn Williams as a centre was the jewel in the crown, a player of sheer genius.

I was astonished to discover that even in the Mecca of rugby, players were left to their own devices in training. It was just as I had experienced in West Wales two years previously. Those were the days when many forwards had big waistlines – fitness had yet to be popularised.

Mr Brice Jenkins, the club secretary, insisted that all players, even the great Haydn Tanner, had to submit a written request to play for the club.

Money was an invisible commodity in the club. It never went into players' pockets unless a receipt, bus or train ticket was given as evidence of a journey. I remember on one occasion using a taxi from Bridgend for a certain Second XV match whereupon, on my producing a receipt, Mr Jenkins paid the fare without batting an eyelid.

The main attraction of the club was probably its style. It went about its business with ostentation. All the players carried it, the First XV and the Second XV. It was probably the only club in Great Britain to provide a cask of free beer to both teams for a home game. There were Aberdeen kippers and a cup of tea after each training period. There was first-class travel and accommodation for away games. There were club functions, dinners, dances, outings and ladies' nights, and the annual tour to Devon and Cornwall. No wonder many appeared in the trials.

I played enough rugby to get my Rags cap (Cardiff's Second XV) and I also played on occasion in the First XV. Probably my nearest claim to fame was being called by Mr Brice Jenkins as reserve for the Cardiff v. New Zealand game of 1953 when Cardiff sensationally beat the All Blacks.

The support for Welsh club rugby at this time was at its highest, and at Cardiff it was overwhelming. To gain entry into the social club at the Arms Park after a game was nigh-on impossible; it would have been easier to enter Fort Knox.

In the dead of winter, when the matches used to finish early, around four o'clock, there was always a spontaneous sing-song with both teams providing entertainers from their own ranks. It was said that some clubs, perhaps left with a split vote over a position during the team selection, would resolve the problem by the chairman casting his vote for the one who could make a better contribution to the social evening.

I had experienced these social nights before on my visits to Cardiff and the tradition had remained, resulting in bawdiness and loud singing before the end of the evening. Now that I was more mature I became more philosophical and the scene did not impress me as before. It was then I realised that not all players were involved in drinking and in the sing-song. There were many VIPs present: gentlemen of the press, business, the BBC, education, NCB, SCOW, civil servants – all keen rugby supporters. Many of them were not averse to using their power to provide a better job to a rugby star who in turn was prepared to reciprocate by infiltrating them into the Welsh rugby scene, especially at international level. All doors opened if one was in the company of one of the top rugby stars.

I cannot blame the rugby superstars for using their rugby talent to further their own job interest. They chose to play amateur rugby and gave pleasure to millions in so doing. A good job for life was a just reward for providing so much enjoyment to the rugby supporters.

Cardiff is the Mecca of Welsh rugby, there is no doubt about that. As much as we in the west, Llanelli and Swansea in particular, used to grumble about Cardiff being the location of the national stadium, nowadays that protest has dissipated to a whisper. I enjoyed the Cardiff experience. I was grateful to Bleddyn Williams for being honoured to play for his distinguished XV at Rydal School and Mountain Ash.

My time in Cardiff was rapidly coming to an end. I applied for a job in Ruthin, North Wales, and as destiny would have it the post was given to a North Walian. England offered the most scope, but I was determined to procure a job in a Welsh-speaking area. Searching through the *Western Mail*, I spotted an advert for a PE man with general subjects at the Boys' Secondary Technical School and College of Further Education, Pontardawe, in the Swansea Valley, only six miles from where I had lived in Craig-cefn-parc.

Pontardawe could at one time claim to be one of the most successful rugby clubs in Wales. In 1920 they achieved notable victories over the giants of West Wales: Llanelli, Aberavon, Swansea and Neath. Unfortunately, many of their players, because of the industrial depression of the '20s and '30s, had to cross Offa's Dyke, where the fact that they had played rugby for Pontardawe was considered by border English clubs as a recommendation worthy of providing them with jobs as long as they played for them.

Pontardawe's first cap was Phil Hopkin in 1908. He had the

distinction of being in the first ever Welsh XV to play at Twickenham, in 1910.

Billiards and snooker were very popular too and were played to a very high standard. Two local lads, Ritchie Smith and Jackie Carney, were at one time British Boys Snooker Champions.

The Swansea Valley has always been conscious of the value of education. In 1953 they could claim two grammar schools, a secondary technical school which housed a small college of further education, and three secondary modern schools. The Tech, as it was popularly known, was built in response to the demands of local industry. So supportive of its establishment were they that they grant-aided its construction, so as to ensure that future generations of young people would have technical and commercial training. It was an academy not for learning, but for living. It was such a success that, at a later date, parents from the Gower area insisted that the technical scholarship examination should include their boys as well, despite the fact that many of them had to travel over sixty miles to and from school. The results of the entrance examination showed how ludicrous pupil assessment was at that time. One would have thought that the results of the examination would be confined to the 'A' streams of the secondary modern schools, but boys from the 'B' and 'C' streams took a share as well. It was a school for no-hopers, 11+ failures and second-chance boys. All the brains, so the academics decreed, had been absorbed into the grammar school, and what was left was given a lifeline in a desperate final attempt to achieve glory by passing the technical school scholarship. In contemporary terms they would have been placed in the lower-middle band of a large comprehensive school, barely capable of sitting GCSE examinations.

The headmaster of the secondary technical school, Mr Oswald Thomas, OBE, MSc, fondly called 'Ossie' by the boys behind his back, was completely unorthodox. He believed in boys 'getting on'. He realised that they should be trained to make a living and that without technological and commercial skills the country would starve. He often boosted the boys' morale by insisting that one failure, in their case the 11+, did not necessarily mean disaster.

Mr Thomas had arrived in the school a term before me, to find it efficient in supplying the needs of local industry in training apprentices. He dropped a bombshell one day when he said, 'It is my intention, in this school, to change the emphasis from craft to technology.' This produced a furore of opposition. 'You can't do that, Mr Thomas. Our boys are 11+ failures.' He was too wily for them. 'There are three 11+ failures and three grammar school rejects on this staff alone. If you can do it, they can too!' he said with conviction. He was aware that his staff possessed a deep sense of vocation and that a school was a place for work and happiness. Four of us who had worked in the mines, Ken Edwards, Tom Jenkins, Glyn Lloyd and myself, and Edwin Clement, a baker's roundsman, were products of the Tech's night-school. John McCloed was an ex-RAF officer graduate. The teachers of English and Welsh, however, changed very often and were products of the University of Wales: Cyril Lewis, Len Evans, Crad Owen, Cynog Dafis, later a Plaid Cymru MP, and Gareth Jones.

'I have decided that in July of next year our final-year pupils will sit 'O' level in maths, engineering science, woodwork, engineering and technical drawing, and workshop technology,' he proclaimed with confidence.

'It's hardly credible that you want us to do a three-year course in one year, with inferior boys. It's impossible!' implored an agitated teacher. 'They are not inferior,' Mr Thomas retorted angrily. 'I have faith in them. Do I have your support or not?'

When the results of the 'O' level exams were announced the following August, the boys had surpassed themselves. The headmaster and his staff were really ecstatic. But Mr Thomas was still not satisfied. The following year he added English language and literature, scripture, Welsh and special arithmetic, to make a formidable list of ten subjects in all. In fairness, the results on occasions were really outstanding, with some of the boys achieving passes in ten subjects. I am unaware of how he succeeded in involving the other teachers in the examination, but it's worth citing my own case.

When I examined my timetable, I discovered that I had been allocated six lessons of scripture. The only reason for designating me to that subject was the fact that it had been decided that the most recently appointed teacher, in this case me, would be responsible for its teaching. Much to my delight, I found that it was not an examinable subject and, as I gained confidence, I found a formula in the teaching of Christian and games ethics simultaneously.

'Let another man praise thee, and not thine own mouth.' The referee is right even though he is wrong.

'Where there is no vision, the people perish.' Be sympathetic to an injured player.

'The ants are a people not strong, yet they prepare their meat in the summer.' It is necessary for the players and the team to practise beforehand.

The response to such topics as modesty, referees' decisions, gaps in opponents' defences, sympathy and preparation before playing became the most popular lessons of the week.

Our happiness and contentment had been observed by Mr Thomas. He called me to his room one day.

'How do you manage to create such interest in a difficult subject like scripture?' he asked quite seriously.

I could not tell him the truth, for I was sure he would be displeased with our more recent topics ('Would you send off a player for swearing?' and 'What should a prop do if the opponent's second-row forward is discreetly contemplating closing his other eye?').

'I notice you do not use exercise and text books – and yet you manage to sustain interest.'

'There are fabulous stories in the Bible.'

'Yes, I know. What are your qualifications in the subject?'

'None at all. Just the fact that I attended Sunday School regularly at one time,' I said quite innocently.

'I knew it! I knew it!' he exclaimed excitedly, jumping to his feet. 'Just the very person to take 'O' level scripture with the boys.'

I was staggered. I protested, but it was to no avail. I left his room in a daze, with the scripture syllabus in my hand. I was worried about the prospect, but much to my surprise and my relief some of the boys did pass. I found that encouraging. It boosted my morale for continuing with the subject during the time I was in the school.

It would be a futile exercise to list the achievements of those 'no-hopers'. They are to be found holding responsible posts in industry and education and as self-employed business entrepreneurs, and their results at the Tech make a mockery of the current system of education.

Mr Thomas doted on rugby. His only real claim to fame in the sport was that he played wing three-quarter alongside the great Claude Davey, the former redoubtable captain of Wales, who had the distinction of being included in two sides, Swansea and Wales, to beat the 1935 New Zealand tourists, scoring three tries in his endeavours. He was also included in the Welsh XV that won at Twickenham for the first time.

Claude was Mr Thomas's hero. He had made a big impression on him, and his association with Claude made him a devout disciple of the game. In consequence, the boys had to bring kit to the Tech; it would not be an exaggeration to say that it became his personal regulation. Many an unwilling boy started and continued playing rugby on account of his keenness.

I remember an irate widow coming to school one day, insisting that her only child was not to play the 'barbaric game'. Mr Thomas tried to make her 'see sense', as he said to me afterwards, but the woman was determined and pleaded with the school governors. They, however, remained steadfast in their support of the headmaster. The boy was more or less coerced into playing – and once he started, he did not stop until he was in his mid-thirties. Rugby became such an obsession with him that he has maintained his involvement with the game as secretary of a rugby club.

Mr Thomas had a great sense of compassion for and empathy with asthma sufferers. It was quite a coincidence that three young sufferers came to school in the same year. Their complaint automatically debarred them from PE. The majority of headmasters would have accepted the fact – but not Mr Thomas. He arranged for the boys' fathers to visit him after school one day. He asked each one, in turn, to relate the history of his son's asthma. 'My boy fell into the Swansea Valley canal when he was five. He could not swim, see, and had a fright. He's had a bad chest ever since,' said one. 'John has had over a hundred injections for his asthma,' blurted the second. The third stated quite simply, 'He was born with it.'

Mr Thomas pondered for a moment. 'I have asked Mr Samuel to take them in PE and he's agreed.'

'But they've got asthma,' they chorused.

'So have I,' Mr Thomas said, breathing heavily. 'That's my one regret in life. Sitting for years in a school gymnasium, while the other boys were exercised to be strong and healthy.' The revelation of his own experiences did the trick.

From the first day the three boys donned their kit, they blossomed.

It seemed as if they had been released from a long period of captivity, where they had been daily victims of warm clothing, injections and pills. The three played rugby. One played regularly for one of the top three first-class rugby clubs in Wales. Another won a Welsh Youth cap, and the third played outside-half in the tough West Wales League.

In addition to being headmaster of the technical secondary school, Mr Thomas was also principal of the college of further education. One of its most famous student apprentices was the great troubadour Max Boyce, who studied electrical engineering there before he won fame and fortune as an entertainer in the golden era of Welsh rugby. It is difficult to convey the day-to-day atmosphere of the whole establishment under the headship of Mr Thomas. His devotion to the job was unparalleled. He started every day at eight thirty and finished at nine every night. He even visited the school on Christmas Day. He never descended to physical punishment, but always appealed to the miscreant's honesty, stressing the principle of 'On my honour I won't'.

His methods of punishment too were completely unorthodox. I recall one particular incident with great enjoyment. Two boys, Gwilym and Adrian, had been excused by their teacher to go to the toilet. When they got to the school's main corridor, they found it very quiet and clear of people. One decided to break wind loud and clear, whilst the other laughed and joined in to make a duet as they made their way to the toilet. Much to their astonishment and sheer terror, who came out but 'Ossie' himself. The boys stopped dead in their tracks.

'Oh, breaking wind in public is it?'

The boys, shamefaced, stood with heads down.

'You'd better go to the toilet and afterwards go and stand outside the door of my room, while I mix a little something for your poor stomachs.'

The boys, crestfallen, followed the head's instructions.

Some time later, who came out of the chemistry laboratory holding two beakers of a sinister-looking liquid but the headmaster, who proceeded towards his study. Once inside, he placed the beakers on his desk, and told the boys to enter. 'Take one each and drink it down!' he commanded.

The boys hesitated.

'Drink it!' The headmaster's tone had changed.

With great reluctance, the boys gulped the concoction down with apparent distaste.

'You'll feel better after that, because I have mixed for you . . .', and he listed a combination of chemical terms which added to the boys' distress. They looked like ghosts for the rest of the day.

The story did not end there, for some ten years later, when Gareth Edwards made his debut for Wales in France, I met Adrian in the Montmartre area of Paris. He recounted that story and sorrowfully recited how ill he and Gwilym had been that morning after taking 'Ossie's' mysterious potion. When I told him that the concoction was only milk and water, he would not believe it.

Despite the enthusiasm for sport, the facilities for physical education in the Tech were non-existent. What we did have was at the discretion of the grammar school. The games field was a walk of a mile from the school. The rugby pitch allocated to us was half a normal pitch. The zinc changing-room was an insult. It was equipped to take thirty boys, but at times over a hundred tried to change there. It was a hopeless situation which forced the majority of boys to change outside. To add to the hopelessness, stacks of artificial manure occupied the middle of the shed. There were no flush-toilets, just open buckets. No water, just an outside tap. The place reeked of disinfectant. But, despite shortcomings, it was there that we practised our rugby and athletics in 1953. It was so different from what I experienced later when I saw independent schools in England with as many as eighteen full-size rugby pitches. If it rained, as it often did, the boys would have to change and run up the side of the valley carrying a satchel and a kit bag to catch a school bus to take them home, some as far as thirty miles.

I will never forget my first lesson in the gymnasium. I had always been aware of my inadequacies as a gymnast, so it was quite natural for me to be nervous and apprehensive in my first real test as a teacher of gymnastics. After the boys had changed, I opened the gym door to allow the first boy in line to enter. A miniature Tarzan in appearance, he ran flat out into the centre of the gym, turned a somersault, landed, executed a hand-spring and then, with apparent ease, walked around the gym on his hands and came to a stop by my feet, as much as to say, 'Beat that.' I was stunned. How many more like him? Luckily he was the only one, or I should have been redundant there and then. It transpired that he was Ronnie James, the boy whom I mentioned earlier for his kicking prowess, who belonged to the James family of Ystalyfera, renowned immediately before the last war for their gymnastic ability.

After a few weeks of teaching I knew that I had found my true vocation. I vowed that all the boys in my charge would get every opportunity to at least improve their health and physical fitness and be taught to play properly, and not suffer, as my generation had, from inadequate physical education. There were only ninety boys, aged from thirteen and a half to seventeen, in the school, probably the smallest secondary school in Wales. With such a small number and such a diversity of ages I could have opted out of inter-school games, but I did not – the best decision I ever made. Playing pick-up sides would have resulted in a boring and frustrating chore for both master and boys. Although I had played rugby in all the positions in the backs except half-back, I realised that I hardly knew anything about, for example, scrum-half or hooker. How could I teach positions which were foreign to me? I had taken the WRU Coaching Certificate in 1953 – only to discover that we knew more than the ex-internationals who were acting as examiners! To satisfy my own knowledge I read every available book on rugby. I questioned every rugby master I respected, and spoke to players of every level, first and second class, internationals, British Lions and even referees. In this way I became a better teacher.

One of the first serious problems I encountered was the problem of the small boy. What to do with him? The first time I took the school team away to play in a match, a colleague had picked the team, because I did not know the pupils well enough. I noticed a boy who was clearly too small to play. When I questioned him I discovered that he was playing at scrum-half. I muttered to myself, 'Make the most of it, son. You won't be playing again.' I soon regretted my words. Brian Edwards proved himself to be an encyclopaedia of rugby skills. That one experience taught me that a small boy can be a priceless acquisition.

Those were halcyon days when one could more or less guarantee that a boy would not be injured providing he learnt his lessons properly. 'Rest your head on his buttocks when you side-tackle.' 'Fall properly on the ball in a forward rush. Not too early, or late! A dirty player will kick your back blue.'

It was not long before rugby became a religion in the school, with teachers forever complaining that the boys were always late from break periods, so captivated were they with rugby football. They would do anything for a game. They were driven with enthusiastic compulsion to become better, to seek perfection. Only a minimum number of players could achieve that goal, but there was one boy who would join their ranks and emerge a superstar from the primitive and humble facilities that existed in the Tech at Pontardawe.

Chapter Seven

Boy with Sporting Genius

By the time Gareth Edwards came to school in 1961, I was thoroughly committed to teaching rugby football. Whereas normal teachers would be on the lookout for well-behaved and well-dressed boys, my observations would be of a different kind. My prime occupation would be to hazard a guess at what position on the rugby field would suit each new boy (whether he had played rugby or not did not matter). By the time I had seen them working in the gym and on the rugby field a few times, I was confident that I could place them in their correct team positions for the rest of their playing days.

One of my first rugby duties every year in September was to discover which boys wanted to appear in the Swansea Valley District Rugby Union Under-Fifteen trials. As usual, I placed a plain piece of paper on the rugby notice-board inviting the boys who were eligible, and thought themselves good enough, to place their name, position, weight and height on the notice-board. In due course, I took the list down and noticed that Gareth's name was above the rest. He claimed he was a centre, eight stone five pounds, and five feet three inches. 'He'll never make the team,' I thought.

The following Saturday morning, with other members of the committee, I was on the touchline observing the trialists in action. It was a very good trial, with plenty of exciting talent on view. The three-quarters were big boys. It was quite evident that Gareth was Lilliputian in comparison and in imminent danger of being hurt. Without any prompting from me, he was told by a wise master to come off the field. He had shown plenty of spirit but his withdrawal had obviously disappointed him. He came towards me very dejectedly.

'Paid â becso, boi bach. Daw dy dro di eto,' ('Don't worry, lad, your turn will come again') I said. 'Go and shower. You can come home with me. My car is the red Mini over there,' I said, pointing to where it was parked.

A few hours later I went to my car. He was not there. The following Monday, during morning break, I saw him with his friend, David John, in the school corridor, both eating oranges. I called him over.

'You owe me an apology, don't you?' I asked.

'What have I done wrong, sir?' he asked with surprise.

'I offered you a lift on Saturday. Why didn't you come to say that you were going home?'

'I felt so ashamed. The boys had been running around me as if I had been standing still. When I tried to tackle, they brushed me aside as if I wasn't there. I did not realise that rugby was a big boys' game.'

'Why did you elect to play centre?'

'My rugby hero is Bleddyn Williams, the great Welsh centre. I want to be like him.'

'It's like a Pembrokeshire corgi wanting to be a sheep-dog. It can't be done. At this moment you are too small to play in midfield.'

'That's what I thought. I think I'll concentrate on soccer.' I was taken aback at this seemingly well-rehearsed answer.

'Concentrate on soccer! Not giving in already, boy, are you? Let me remind you that rugby is the game of this school.'

He bowed his head.

'Are you familiar with the Bible, and in particular the Book of Proverbs?'

He looked at me with his mouth agape, astonishment written all over his face.

'"If you are weak in the time of crisis, you are weak indeed",' I said with a big smile.

The quotation relieved the tension and he began to chuckle.

'While you dashed home on Saturday, I stayed to watch the trial through. It's a good job I did because I saw a position which is tailor-made for you. A position you will fill within a month if you listen to me.' I could see the intense curiosity on his face. He could not refrain from blurting out, 'What position is that, Mr Samuel?'

'Have you ever thought of yourself as a scrum-half?'

He pondered for a moment. 'I've never played in that position before, sir.'

'Well, you are never too old to learn, are you? We can start from scratch. I'll make you into one. We have produced many a Swansea Valley scrum-half in our school, you know. We'll start this afternoon in the games lesson, and stay behind for an hour after school. Mark my words, you'll be playing for the district within a month.'

'Thank you, sir. I'll do my best.'

'That's the idea. You can't do better than that.'

As we went our separate ways, he said, 'Sorry about the lift last Saturday. It won't happen again, sir.' With that he gave a huge whoop as he hopped, skipped and jumped down the corridor, with David John in his wake.

That afternoon we started. 'Roll the ball against the goalpost, and on the rebound, pass off the ground to me. Your feet should be wide apart and your outside foot indicating in which direction the ball is to be passed. Keep your back flat and extend your arms and finally flick your wrists as you pass the ball. The rule states you should stand one yard from the scrum and put the ball in at a level between your knee and ankle.' A new scrum-half, and the same annual routine.

He took to the position as a duck to water. Within a month he was the proud and regular scrum-half of the Swansea Valley Schools. He had been hooked and was destined to spend his leisure time practising to play eventually, or so I thought at the time, for Cwmgors, his village club.

Whereas Gareth got into the team by the skin of his teeth, other boys in his form got in by their sheer brilliance. One boy in particular, David Kenyon, eventually captained the Probables at Under-Fifteen level, but for some inexplicable reason was denied a cap.

All kinds of people have been acknowledged by Gareth for helping him on his way. He has failed to recognise, not deliberately I am sure, those who made the biggest contribution to his ultimate success. It is impossible to develop super rugby players unless they experience keen and determined opposition. Gareth's classmates could not have been better if they had been hand-picked. They were a dedicated, fearless and competitive group, many of whom, at that time, were infinitely better than he was because of their size, speed and strength. He had to build up a survival mechanism based on the acquisition of skill, speed and strength.

On occasion, during a games lesson, the opposition was such that an opponent very often scored directly from a kick-out. Gareth was not one of those. In fact, I remember him on one occasion being carried with the ball over the goal-line and the ball being wrestled from him for his opponent to score. In order to retain the interest of both the small and the big boy within this context, special rules had to be implemented to encourage both to enjoy their rugby lessons. There is nothing as soul-destroying for a small boy as attempting to tackle a giant in overdrive. A teacher must, therefore, be alert to the needs of both. In the three years that followed, Gareth Edwards was clobbered time and time again. If I told him beforehand in a practice game to break from the scrum, I would also give a nod to Rodney Williams, wing forward, and Gareth Jones, scrum-half, to provide a reception committee. Therefore when he eventually met the most Herculean of forwards, like Colin Meads, the great New Zealand lock, their sizeable proportions held no fear for him because, relatively speaking, he had always had the big guy around to try and take advantage of him on the playing-field and in the gymnasium.

His early training and his eventual emergence as a ruthless scrum-half with a vision of 360° must be attributed to a large extent to his classmates. The fact that he played over fifty games for Wales without a serious injury testifies to the durability he acquired in sharing the physical education programme with those rather special boys.

I also found that they enjoyed playing rugby league as a diversion from the normal rugby lesson. Its uncomplicated nature, wide spaces and boy-to-boy tackling appealed to their competitive instincts.

Gareth's introductory season with the Swansea Valley Schoolboys was not startling. He did not reveal any promise at all. He was just a small, run-of-the-mill schoolboy scrum-half.

However, if he was not a good rugby player, he was certainly a brilliant gymnast. His greatest asset was his uncanny ability to learn new physical movements without any trouble at all. He was the star performer in the group when the Tech's gymnastic team gave a display on BBC Wales. I remember a St David's Day Eisteddfod when we used to hold an inter-house 'walking on hands for the longest distance' competition. In previous years the competition had ended inside the hall, but when Gareth's turn came I had to open the door for him to continue hand-walking down the corridor and outside to the yard, whereupon I had to stop him. When he reappeared in the hall he received thunderous applause.

During the next three years, in addition to gymnastics, he shared with his classmates a very rigorous programme of circuit, target and weight training. The rivalry was intense and the performances were really extraordinary. Physical education was acknowledged as a very important subject in the school and accordingly end-of-term marks were given on a parity with the other subjects, the only school in Glamorgan to operate such a system. He also practised gymnastics as an after-school activity on Monday evenings for the purpose of competing in the Urdd National Eisteddfod.

When the summer of 1962 came, I prepared for the athletics season. I could not teach cricket because we had no facilities; consequently I concentrated on athletics, without a doubt the finest training for prospective rugby players. I used to recommend those who had ambitions in cricket to the many village cricket clubs available in the area, with the result that none of them missed the experience of playing the game.

The old county of Glamorgan believed in athletics. Even the director of education, Trevor Jenkins, Esq., was enthusiastic in his support. He used to come and judge one of the events in the County Championships. Every child who was prepared to make an extra effort was awarded a County Certificate if he achieved certain standards in the athletics event of his choice. These certificates were highly respected tokens of achievement. Athletics is a multi-sport where it is possible for a child to derive pleasure from running, throwing or jumping. It is a fundamental and satisfying sport which offers no easy options. It is also a tough sport, which produces speed, strength, stamina and suppleness, the ingredients necessary to produce the best-quality rugby players.

When I had completed my first athletics lesson with Gareth's class, I was thoroughly exhilarated by their attitude. During the course of the lesson, I had been impressed by a number of them and invited them to stay after school for special tuition and practice.

I was occupied in teaching a particular boy when I noticed Gareth, with his kit bag in one hand and his satchel in the other, running in the direction of the school. 'Hey,' I said. 'Where do you think you are going? Come here!' He reluctantly stopped, dropped his bags, hesitated and came trotting over to me. 'I thought we had agreed that you were to stay for extra practice.'

'But I can out-jump anybody in my class, sir,' he said sheepishly.

'And so you can. The boys who stay behind with me are not aiming to be champions of their class, or Gwaun-cae-gurwen, boy, but champions of Wales. I don't like boys who admire themselves. Be off with you.' I turned on my heel and left him there, staring ruefully at the ground.

I did not know the sequel of that little episode until years later, when Glan, Gareth's father, told me. 'Oh, yes, he came home fuming and in a sorry state. "That Mr Samuel has a down on me. I could out-jump them all in my class and he asks me of all people to stay for extra practice. He called me something like a big-head. I don't like him and I'm not going to school tomorrow."'

Glan was naturally distressed at his unhappiness and so was Mrs Edwards. 'Go over to Cwmgors and see that bugger,' was her reaction, according to Glan. Fortunately, Glan did not agree to his dear wife's request for retribution; had he done so, he would have been surprised to discover that I was not at all the ogre his son had supposed me to be. In fact, he would have found me in a state of excitement, for his son had shown signs of possessing rare ability which I had hoped to develop in the after-school practice.

By nature I happen to be rather direct in my dealings with people. It is a weakness, perhaps, but a quality that Gareth Edwards very quickly came to comprehend as vital in our future relationship. Another quality which I could claim to possess is that I forgive easily; consequently, on the following morning, I sent for him. When he came, he appeared melancholy, tense and forlorn.

'Do you think you can borrow some kit during today's lunch-time, Gareth? I want to test you in the long-jump pit.' The relief on his face was a joy to see. 'Oh yes, sir, I'll borrow from one of the second-year boys. They've got a games lesson today.'

'See you at twelve fifteen, then.' He was there on time, dressed for the occasion. I gave him some warming-up exercises and measured his run-up for the event. 'Remember,' I said, 'to hit the jumping-off board as hard as you can to get as much height as possible; do a cycling motion and reach as far forward as possible with your feet.'

I could see the determination written on his face as he accomplished his trial jumps. His results were extraordinary. Still not satisfied, I took him to the gymnasium and tested his ability at the vertical jump test, and when he recorded a jump of thirty inches I knew that I had a potential super-athlete on my hands. I kept that secret to myself.

That little squabble about the practice resulted in him changing his attitude. He had clearly not realised that he possessed rare qualities which needed to be brought out. He was nonchalant in his approach and that had to change; he enjoyed a joke, and was far too easy-going. Fortunately for him, I was a relentless taskmaster who did not believe in mollycoddling, wasting time and seeking the boys' popularity by taking soft options in physical education. There was no need to ask him to remain after school to practise thereafter. He realised that, with a one-to-one teaching relationship, he was receiving all the attention and he began to revel in it. When the annual West Glamorgan Schools Athletics Championship was held at Bridgend in 1962, it was an impossible idea to think of winning any team trophies, because in the past they had been monopolised by the big grammar schools. There was no reason to believe that the results would be different that year. But I was quietly confident that some members of the junior athletics team would share the placings in one or two of the events.

However big the fish, they say, a small hook can take its life. Did not the mighty Newport lose at rugby to the small village of Penclawdd? And so it was that day in Bridgend, when the small Pontardawe Tech won the junior trophy from the giant schools of West Glamorgan.

I did not exaggerate when I claimed that Gareth Edwards owed a debt of gratitude to his classmates in Pontardawe. Gareth was very pleased with himself, gaining a first and two second prizes, which was the impetus he needed.

'I really enjoyed that meeting today, Mr Samuel. It's a good job we trained so hard.'

'You are beginning to realise that winning is better than losing, and that taking part is more important than being idle. Your dreams can only be fulfilled by hard work.'

From that moment onwards he trained at least an hour every day. He did not resent training any more; he began to enjoy it, and it became a part of his daily routine. He ended up a county champion – a modest beginning.

With this success his relationship with me changed. He seemed to realise that if he wanted to achieve something worthwhile, it was best to keep close to me. He could not help being close to me, anyway, for I taught him maths, English, scripture and PE, nearly half his weekly school timetable. In addition, he was a member of my Urdd gymnastic club, and also attended the Gwaun-cae-gurwen youth club twice a week, where I was warden. He also followed my schedules during school holidays and weekends.

His emergence as a promising athlete was spotted by the late Matt Cullen, an exiled Irishman who lived in Clydach. Matt had an uncontrolled passion for athletics. Every weekend he used to enjoy taking, at his own expense, a van-load of the best young athletes in the Swansea Valley to athletics meetings all over South Wales. Generations of young people in the area enjoyed Matt's benevolence. He was heartbroken when the comprehensive system of education no longer had time for the sport which had been his lifeline. Athletics became too tough for the affluent society.

When Gareth returned for his second year he was a changed young man. His athletics, as far as I was concerned, were in the distant past, for it was the rugby season once again.

'It does not matter where you go; if you play rugby, you are assured of making friends. Be it university, college, factory or staying in your village, rugby is a universal brotherhood,' I used to say to them in class when the rain had intervened to stop our rugby lessons. The free periods would always involve talks about the many facets of rugby. All would listen and make a contribution to the theme.

Over the years I developed the knack of acquiring images of the best players in the world performing certain rugby skills. This is what teaching physical skills is about. One has an image of what is needed and then proceeds to teach the individual until the skill is mastered. At the end, one must ask, 'Does he look right according to the image one possesses of the skill to be accomplished?'

For example, I had observed closely the scrum-halfs of my day and I can still picture Haydn Tanner's (Cardiff) swivel-pass; Roy Sutton's (Swansea) full-arm-extension dummy-pass; Rex Willis's (Cardiff) durability and tenacity; Onllwyn Brace's (Oxford University) dummy-scissors; and Goronwy Morgan's (St Luke's) blind-side break. In addition, there was the unheralded Les James (Vardre, Trebanos, Glais), an excellent West Wales League scrum-half who knew all the tricks about the position, good and bad.

With this fund of knowledge I had often wondered if it was possible to mould a scrum-half with a combination of the aforementioned virtues and also to make one superior to them all, possessing more strength, speed and skill. I was aware that there was a need to expand the position's role. It had remained too static, and needed to extend its role and to reveal more involvement and athleticism during the game. There was an abundance of scrum-halfs who could pass a ball, but not many blessed with the vision needed to enlarge the position's unlimited scope.

Not that I was thinking along those lines for the young Gareth in those months of 1962. He appeared in a Welsh secondary schools' trial at that period and was rightly eliminated. He became a puzzle to me. I never experienced a boy who could absorb the teaching of skill so easily. Nothing deterred him. Having proved himself as a gymnast and an athlete, he was beginning to shine as a scrum-half. The trial had proved to me that, within a year, he would be a serious candidate for a secondary schools' cap. I was inwardly confident of that. It was during an after-school practice that I was finally convinced that he had the ability to become a great player.

There are over twenty different kinds of kick in rugby football, not all of them easy. The one I wanted to teach Gareth was the kick in defence from a lineout near the goal-line and under extreme pressure. It is a very difficult kick, which only a few of the current international scrum-halfs can accomplish properly. Gareth had arranged for his friend, David John, to stay behind to help us with the practice.

'It is your job, David John, to throw the ball to me while I am standing in the lineout as a second-row forward,' I said in a convincing tone. 'As soon as I pass it to you, Gareth, at scrum-half, I become a loose forward whose job it is to stop you from kicking the ball into touch. Got it? Right! Throw the ball then, David John!'

We did the practice twice. On each occasion I smothered Gareth's attempts at kicking into touch and made sure that I roughed him up a bit. 'Not much shape in this one kicking the ball, David John,' I said. David John refused to comment. It was no use asking him whose side he was on. 'Are you ready? Let's have it again.'

Before the ball was thrown, I had a look at Gareth. There was a mixture of anger and determination on his face. He was on the verge of losing his temper. I smiled at the prospect. We remained motionless until David John spurred us into action. The ball was in Gareth's hands before he knew it, and while he was in the process of kicking the ball I was on him like a ton of bricks, just enough to test his reaction.

I helped him to his feet as he released a torrent of expletives. 'That's not fair! You did not give me a chance,' he cried.

'Hold on now, boy. Don't lose your temper. That's a bad sign,' I replied in a firm tone. 'Let me play scrum-half so that I can show you how it's done.'

Suddenly his whole attitude changed. His personal tirade against me finished. The chance he wanted for revenge had been offered to him. His whole being expressed his resolution; he was going to knock Bill Samuel for six. Fourteen stone or not, it did not matter.

David John was taking more than a passing interest in the exchanges. I heard him whisper, 'Bwr e lawr' ('Knock him down'). Both of them were ready.

The ball was thrown, caught and passed to me by Gareth and, at the same time, with nostrils aflame, he came thundering towards me. Too late; the ball had been kicked and was sailing sweetly down the touchline to land in touch forty yards away. Gareth stopped in his tracks, and his face broke into a smile. 'Oh, is that the way you do it?' he said, with a big laugh.

He would then be anxious to experiment and practise the art himself. This he would do for weeks on end, and when he had achieved a standard of competency, I would take him to the left-side touchline and encourage him to practise kicking in the same situation with his left foot. All his practices were for real. On other occasions, after certain practices, I would say, 'Oh, Gareth, that's it. Let's do the kicking-at-goal practice before we go home. Twelve times this time.'

'Oh, come on, Mr Samuel, must I go through that practice again?'

'The sooner the better. I want to go home too. My dinner will be on the hob by this time.'

We would collect all the rugby balls and drop them near where one of the corner flags would be. He would then proceed to dig a hole with his heel, place ball after ball and kick each one at the nearest single goalpost, whilst I gathered and kicked them back. When he had hit his target a dozen times he would call it a day.

His talent was manifesting itself all the time. He was completely unaware of the change that had occurred in him. It was too good to be true. Did I have a prospective rugby star on my hands, as well as a brilliant gymnast and athlete? While I was planning things for him to do, I discovered that Swansea Town were showing an interest in signing him as an apprentice. I had been told that he was the star soccer player of the village team. I was quietly pleased, because he was developing skills which would be invaluable to him as a rugby player. He did not confide in me, or provide me with information regarding the rumour. His whole attitude changed. He became furtive and independent. Whereas before he had been forthcoming, cordial and fun-loving, he became truculent and less conspicuous in his physical activities. The situation had to be resolved, because the glamour of soccer was like a magnet to him and his loyalty to the school was making him unhappy.

During one of Gareth's uncommunicative days I spoke to him. 'Do you think it would help if I spoke to you and your parents about your prospects in soccer?'

He was taken aback at the proposition, but he wisely agreed to a meeting. It was my first visit to 53 Colbren Square, the cosy home of Mr and Mrs Glan Edwards. Sitting comfortably around a bright coal fire, drinking cups of tea, we discussed at length the choice they would inevitably have to make. Mr and Mrs Edwards had no real opinions on the matter, wanting the boy to make sure that he chose the right option.

'I have no objection to Gareth becoming a soccer apprentice,' I assured them. 'It would suit Gareth perfectly. No more schooling. An idyllic existence.' I warmed to my theme as Gareth stood transfixed, ready to listen to every word.

'Ever since I have been in the Tech, I have seen excited boys going on trials to some of the top clubs in the country. Not one of them made the grade. I am a qualified soccer coach and referee. What would Manchester United do if I recommended a promising boy to them? Not only would they thank me, they'd send me a cheque as well, providing the boy was any good. Name your club, Gareth. I'll fix a trial period for you.'

'What would *you* do, Mr Samuel, if he were *your* boy?' intervened Mrs Edwards, with the concern of a proud and caring mother.

'I am sorry, Mrs Edwards – he must make that decision for himself. I can write on his behalf to Manchester United, Arsenal, Spurs. Or, he can work for his 'O' levels to become a PE teacher, and play rugby for Wales.'

'Play rugby for Wales, indeed! He'll be lucky to play for Cwmgors,' they both scoffed.

'You mark my words,' I said, having foolishly expressed my inner thoughts.

As anticipated, they opted, as thousands of Welsh parents had done before them, for security. Mrs Edwards, in deadly earnest, said, 'He'd better pitch in at school from now on. It's up to him now.'

'It's up to him.' The words echoed in my ears as I walked homewards. I could not help thinking, 'Aye, and up to me too! Fancy scoffing at my prophecy of Gareth playing for Wales. I must be careful or people will think I'm daft.'

Once the matter of soccer had been resolved, he continued with his Herculean programme and, happily, our harmonious relationship was restored.

Others did not share my view that he was a budding scrum-half. He was selected for Cwmgors Youth as a hooker, preference being given to S4C's rugby commentator Huw Llewelyn Davies, whose father, Eic, was one of the pioneers of Welsh-language sports programmes. Huw enjoys the distinction of being chosen to play in the scrum-half position instead of Gareth.

It was in athletics that he began to be noticed. His versatility was phenomenal, particularly in pole-vaulting. One afternoon he cleared

10ft 6ins with an aluminium pole into a not-too-sandy pit. I became really frightened, and refused to have the bar any higher, for I did not possess the expertise to coach him. He was chosen to join an élite group to be coached by the then Welsh National Athletics Coach, Mr Ron Pickering, BBC athletics commentator. I wrote to him, informing him of Gareth's potential in pole-vaulting. It transpired that the athletes specialised in sprinting and jumping and that no provision had been made for the coaching of pole-vaulting. Mr Pickering tried to help by giving him a book on pole-vaulting. I have always considered that Gareth could have represented Britain in that event.

Even though we had only one hurdle at school, I decided to make him into a hurdler because of its similarity to the running of a scrum-half. Both need explosive starts from a bent position, considerable pace over or around obstacles and a final surge in achieving the goal, or finishing line. With only one hurdle available, we had to measure distances between the supposed hurdles and then place a coat where each hurdle should be. Fortunately, because of Gareth's success, that laborious arrangement did not last long. He became Welsh Secondary Schools 200 yards Low Hurdles and Welsh Games Long Jump Champion in 1963. What had started out innocently as rugby training resulted in the discovery of a rare talent in athletics.

It was by accident I found the ideal training-circuit for young athletes. Not far from the school, there were a hundred and ninety steps on the most forbidding gradient imaginable. It was there, on the steps to the Pontardawe Golf Club, that Gareth exercised his legs and improved his lung capacity. The course started on the flat near the school, followed by an embankment, and then the steps. His best performance was twelve times during lunch-time, when most of the school was there to watch him. He did that in a normal school lunch-hour, which included changing, a shower and a school lunch. Ten years later I challenged the Cwmtawe First XV squad to have a go at it, so as to test their fitness. Most of them managed three circuits, and the best performer on the day achieved six.

Gareth had experienced a wonderful season of athletics and came back to school for his third and final year in 1963–64. It was a crucial year for him, with nine 'O' levels to sit and, as far as I was concerned, the preparation for a Schoolboy cap at the Under-Nineteen Level. He was sixteen at the time and full of the exuberance of youth. His individuality became more apparent as he continued to improve on the basic skills of side-stepping, dodging and swerving around his opponents, more often than not leaving them standing with the suddenness and unexpectedness of his changes of direction. He relied more on body than on brain. Very often he played like a whirlabout without any control at all. It was my job to slow him down so as to introduce subtlety and innovation, as well as to instil in him unselfishness and judgement, the hallmark of all great players in any sport.

I will always remember his first trial, in Pontardawe. Two of the Mid-Glamorgan selection committee were present, Val Antolin of Dyfrryn School and John Rees of Garw Grammar. Both were immediately impressed with Gareth's initial play.

'Blimey!' said Val in disbelief. 'Who is that scrum-half? What a pass!'

On that day's performance, he was selected for the next trial, which posed a problem. He needed match practice, and since the Tech was too small to take on the bigger schools, I had no alternative but to ask John Morgan, the rugby master at Pontardawe Grammar, if he would include him in his team to play the following Saturday against Gwendraeth Grammar. Much to my relief, John agreed.

In the meantime, my brother-in-law Tom, married to my sister Dilys, who farmed at Porthyrhyd Farm, not far away from the Gwendraeth School, told me about a new schoolboy rugby phenomenon. 'They haven't seen his like,' said Tom to me. 'He has caused great excitement in the area with his extraordinary rugby talent. All he does is kick the ball. Touch-kicks, drop-kicks, punts, garryowens, kicks to the wing, kicks ahead, cross-kicks and kicks for goal. He's a master. The only time he passes is when he is in the opponents' twenty-five, but almost invariably it will be a drop-goal or a kick to his wings, and usually they are spot on. Very rarely does his team lose. He is a one-man band – well worth seeing.'

Tom was not prone to exaggeration but in this case I thought he had stretched it a bit, but he was right. The boy performed exactly as was predicted. He kicked and kicked, and two of his kicks ahead resulted in tries being scored, and he then kicked the goals with unruffled ease. It was a fascinating performance, but surely it did not help the cause of the three-quarters?

'I've talked to them about it,' said Ray Williams (Llanelli and Wales), Gwendraeth's rugby master, 'but they are happy to be on the winning side, such is his dominance.'

'There's no need to change him, Ray,' I said. 'He's a genius. Tie yourself to his star. He's got a glorious future.'

That was the first time that Barry John and Gareth Edwards appeared on the same pitch. Barry caught the eye that day, but Gareth signalled his presence very much in the minor key by scoring a try.

Barry's singular method of kicking for position in the opponents' twenty-five was not acceptable to the Schools selectors, who thought that his play was contrary to the spirit of schoolboy rugby. I had taken Tech boys to the final trial before, but with Gareth it was different. It would take a very good boy to topple him. He had been chosen to play in the second half and by that time the players had been juggled to make the Reds into what was considered to be the eventual Welsh team. The writing was on the wall. The Reds won most of the possession from scrums and lineouts, leaving Gareth clutching at straws. His dreams died in the depths of despair.

I was so disappointed I did not have the courage to commiserate with him when the trial was over. Nor did I have any objections to the scrum-halfs who were in favour. The best of luck to them, but I felt very strongly about the treatment meted out to him.

However, when Gareth came to me after changing, I said, 'You did not get much chance, did you?'

'Much chance! You must be joking.' He expressed his emotions bitterly. 'What's the point of a trial, if everyone does not get a fair chance to show what he can do?'

'Perhaps you should go to a fashionable grammar school. Not a small insignificant place like the Tech.'

'Dim diolch! No thanks!'

The Glamorgan County Rugby XV recognised him as a player who could play anywhere. He emerged as the man of the match when he played full-back for them against Munster. That was his finale in rugby terms, as far as the Tech was concerned. He had appeared in the final trial of the Welsh Secondary Schools Under-Nineteen group at just over sixteen and a half, which was in itself an achievement, for, after all, he had played only one game of senior schoolboy rugby in his short career as a player.

That summer Gareth excelled himself in athletics and created a new Welsh record for the 200 yards hurdles at Aberystwyth. I had travelled early to be on time for the heats and was alarmed to discover that the road was temporarily blocked at Lampeter owing to repairs. This delay caused me some anxiety, because I did not want to miss the heats, particularly the 200 yards hurdles. Striving through a throng of people outside the stadium's gate, I met a colleague from another school.

'Have the heats for the 200 yards hurdles gone yet?'

'Yes,' said he, 'they have just finished.'

'Did Gareth qualify?' I asked urgently.

'I don't think so,' he replied.

Disconsolately I slowed down and began to feel guilty. It was impossible for him not to have qualified, I said to myself. The Welsh record was in his grasp. He must have fallen over a hurdle. That's it! Was it the school's fault in only providing us with one hurdle instead of ten? No wonder he had not qualified! 'Ye of little faith!', however, is a popular biblical verse – and so it was on that day. The man had made a mistake, and had mixed up the 200 yards with the 110 yards hurdles race.

After walking around and watching the sport for a while, I made a point of seeing Gareth to wish him well. 'The favourite is on the inside lane,' I said. 'Catch him up on the stagger. Keep with him, and give it all you've got after you're over the last hurdle. We are here for the record today!' I said convincingly.

'I'll do my best,' he said.

'Good lad! You can do it,' I replied with a reassuring smile.

I positioned myself by the tape in order to see the finish because I was sure it was going to be a close one. One of the hurdlers had already produced a better time than Gareth that season in an official meeting. 'Don't worry about that time,' I said. 'They usually use the town clock to register times in that county.'

While I was ruminating on this, someone nudged me in the ribs. 'Do you mind if I stand by you, Mr Samuel?' asked the cheerful voice of Glan Edwards, 'so that I can take a photograph of the finish with this, you see.' He held up a neat little box-camera.

'You can if you like,' I said. 'But there is a ruling which says that neither the parents of athletes nor their teachers are allowed inside the track. If you want to risk it, it is up to you.'

'I thought you would not mind. Thank you very much, Mr Samuel' – as if I was the only one that mattered. He walked away as if he had not heard my warning.

I watched him for a while adjusting his camera. He peered through the lens standing, sitting down and kneeling. He turned the knobs one way, and then another, mumbling quietly to himself as he dawdled and shuffled around, just like a professional photographer. Finally he went down on one knee, focused his camera in the direction of the starting blocks and clicked the camera to take the most ambitious telescopic shot ever. Almost simultaneously the starting-gun startled some resting seagulls as the hurdlers were put into dynamic motion. It was evident that there were only two athletes in it when they came out of the bend. Gareth had not made up the leeway but he was hurdling perfectly, while his challenger was running with a great deal of composure. Suddenly I was made aware of Glan, who was now in front of me with his camera in hand, shouting at the top of his voice, 'Dere mlan Gareth! Come on Gareth!'

The crowd roared. The two young athletes kept their cool and their rhythm until the last hurdle was safely cleared. Glan was by this time in a frenzy. 'Dere mlan Gareth!' he gasped. At this encouragement, or so it seemed, Gareth drew on his reserve of tenacity to make a final desperate surge which carried him over the line to break the Welsh record. Glan's excitement and his ecstatic joy were felt by all around.

It was very encouraging to see the Edwards family in Aberystwyth, sharing in Gareth's achievement. Little did they dream at that time that very soon he would be the toast of Wales.

In the summer of 1964, he was long jump and 200 yards hurdles champion of Glamorgan and Welsh Schools and also Welsh Games champion in the 110 yards hurdles. He was recognised by the *Western Mail* as the most promising athlete in Wales and was awarded a special trophy at Thompson House, by the Honorable Anthony Berry. His award by the *Western Mail* had wonderful repercussions as far as the future generations of young Swansea Valley sportsmen and women were concerned.

Over the years, I had complained to the boys about the primitive conditions we suffered during games lessons. The ever-prevailing stench of the lavatory buckets and the cramped conditions of the changing facilities had not been forgotten by one old boy. He was brave enough to write to the editor of the *Western Mail* congratulating Pontardawe on producing the most promising athlete and condemning Glamorgan Education Authority for the primitive conditions which he and others had to endure for training. In no time at all a magnificent new pavilion arrived on the games field, equipped with showers, toilets, ante-rooms and space enough to provide meals for both home and away teams. Succeeding generations of Swansea Valley schoolchildren benefited considerably from Gareth's sudden eminence and from the enterprise of an old boy, Adrian Davies, in writing to the press. Gareth began to experience and enjoy local fame.

'Who is he, then?'

'The son of Glan, who drives buses in his spare time, and Annie Mary, who sews. They live near Eic, you know.'

'He is a nice boy. Said hello to me the other day. Very good at jumping the sticks, they say.'

'Remember now, Gareth,' I used to say to him. 'Once you become a champion, things change. People will want to know you. You have become a talking-point, and because you are local, they have an association with you and want to share your success. Your success is their success and your future is theirs as well. You acknowledge them, or they will call you a big-head. If you drink in public, remember to some of them it's the ruin of mankind; make sure it's orangeade. If you were to drink pints, those who saw you might exaggerate – "He was drinking a lot last night, you know!" Public relations are important. It is imperative that you create a good image so that they can be proud of you.' He would listen to my words without an expression on his face. Twenty years ago they made sense; not now, though.

Time was running out; his days at the Tech were rapidly coming to an end. We had come a long way together, and he trusted me absolutely. I had a feeling at one time that if I asked him on a Friday evening after school to run around Wales and be back by Monday morning, he would be sitting by the school gate, panting, waiting for me to arrive at school, and would ask, 'Beth nesa, syr? What next, sir?'

I was loath to see him go, because I knew that the next two years were vital in his development. He could either enter one of the two local grammar schools or seek an apprenticeship with the NCB. I was not happy with either choice, for I had a feeling – a premonition if you like – that there was a school somewhere that would allow him to train three times a day, seven days a week, and follow on from the work I was doing with him.

Chapter Eight

From Tech to Millfield

One day, as I sat alone in the Tech staff room, I happened to pick up a copy of the *Daily Express*. It must have been Providence that guided me to find within its columns a story about a working-class girl who, because of her brilliance in athletics, had gained a special place at the most expensive fee-paying public school in the United Kingdom. The girl's name, of course, was Mary Bignal, and the school, Millfield, in Somerset. It triggered off a wild idea. Surely what had happened to Mary could also happen to Gareth? A member of staff came into the room and I asked him to read the story about Mary. He did so and with a shrug of his shoulders asked, 'Well, what about it?'

'Don't you think Gareth would qualify?' I asked in earnest.

'Mae eisiau mynd â dy ddwr di i Herbert's boi,' he said. My spirits sank immediately. Herbert was a local herbalist who prescribed a cure once he had analysed your urine!

I pondered about the prospect for days. With tongue in cheek, I quietly sought my wife, Velda's, reaction, and to my surprise she said that no harm would ensue from sending an exploratory letter. After many attempts at composing a letter, I finally managed one which had as its theme 'a sports scholarship at Millfield'. I addressed the letter to the headmaster, without even knowing his name. Within four days a reply came through the post. It was from a name which was not unknown to me – R.J.O. Meyer, Esq., MA, the former distinguished cricketer, captain of Somerset County Cricket Club and the then headmaster of Millfield School. They did not provide sports scholarships at Millfield, he outlined in his letter, but he was always interested in helping any boy or girl of great ability who was not having the chance of developing his or her talents to the full. With the letter he had enclosed a thick colourful brochure which in itself was frightening because of its superior quality.

I thumbed briskly through the pages, searching frenziedly for the details of the fees, and was relieved to discover that, even though they were formidable, it was possible that Mr and Mrs Edwards could, with a generous bursary from the school and a little sacrifice, cope with sending their son to Millfield.

Alas, that impression was instantly dispelled when I examined the paragraph more closely, for it said 'per term' and not 'per year' as I had thought initially. My spirits sank. I knew that, however generous the bursary, we could never possibly entertain the difference in cash. I decided to ignore the contents of the brochure and instead I concentrated on submitting to the headmaster a list of Gareth's achievements to date. They were very impressive.

He had been awarded a cup for being the most promising young athlete in Wales. He had played in the final Welsh Youth soccer trial. He was the Welsh record-holder in the 200 yards hurdles. He was the Welsh Schools and Welsh Youth champion at long jump and 110 yards hurdles. He had played rugby for Glamorgan County as a full-back and had appeared in the final Welsh Secondary Schools trial as a scrum-half. I added that, in my opinion, he could, with proper facilities, represent Britain in gymnastics and athletics, and that if he was given the right training he would represent Britain in the Olympics in pole-vaulting and certainly play rugby for Wales. I hesitated just a little before posting the letter, for Gareth's credentials sounded exaggerated, even to myself.

Within a few days a reply came – 'Gareth Edwards sounds a natural for Millfield'. At the time, that was a big boost for my ego, for to my mind the headmaster was handling requests like mine every day. I read the letter the second time, and came across something disturbing. 'You might tell them that the headmaster has offered to find half the fees, and ask whether they, the Edwards family, would consider finding the other half.' If that was not possible, would I write or contact the monied people of Wales for them to consider providing financial support for a young Welsh sportsman to achieve his ultimate potential and to represent Wales?

FROM TECH TO MILLFIELD

The impact of the suggestion did not fully register for a long time. When it did, I realised it was asking me to beg. I did not relish the idea one bit. Nowadays, there would be no guilt complex attached to such a proposition; it would simply be called 'sponsorship'. I have never liked the word 'begging'; in fact, I loathed it. I have seen many broken-down miners and soldiers destined to a life of penny pinching; broken men playing the accordion, trumpet or mouth-organ, begging from people who had nothing to give, who, in turn, with compassion in their hearts, could only offer a cup of tea and a piece of cake. The realisation that I would have to write and speak to monied people for the sake of pursuing an impossible ideal sickened me. I asked myself, why should I care? The boy knew nothing of my troubles on his behalf and probably did not even share my ambitions for him. Why not allow him to stay in Gwaun-cae-gurwen where I could still keep an eye on him?

The following day I decided on a tactic to see whether I could resolve my problem. As usual at break-time he was in the school corridor. 'Can I have a word with you, Gareth, please?' I said.

He came very quickly with a questioning look on his face.

'Which of the two grammar schools are you going to next year, Pontardawe or Ystalyfera?'

'I don't know. Both of them demand four 'O' levels before I can join the sixth year, and that's a bit of a hurdle in itself.'

'You have no other plans?'

'If I fail, I suppose I'll have to seek an apprenticeship somewhere.'

'Would you like to go away?'

'What do you mean, sir?'

'Well, you are a first-class gymnast. The Army PTI course will take you. A police cadet?'

'The forces don't appeal to me really, and, anyway, I'm too short for the police force.'

'The Army Apprentices offer good trades, you know. Or a rugby-playing public school?'

'A rugby-playing public school? A rugby-playing public school! You must be joking,' and he laughed at the absurdity of the suggestion. 'Me, a miner's boy, who lives in a council house, in with those la-di-das? I honestly can't imagine that,' he continued.

'Well, you never know. Let's hope that you get your 'O' levels. Make sure that you pass in my subject.'

As I walked away I realised what a blithering idiot I was. The boy had no aspirations, he was happy as he was. All the fantasies that existed for him were purely of my own making. He had no ambitions of which I was aware. I realised that whatever was going to happen to him in sport and education would be of *my* volition. *I* was his ambition. During the next few days I wrestled with my problem. I did not want to saddle Mr and Mrs Edwards with financial suicide and I wanted to assure them when the occasion arose that the right thing was being done for their boy. To snatch him from his happy working-class home and place him into the most expensive public school in Britain could have woeful, as well as happy and profitable, repercussions.

Perhaps writing a few letters to the monied people of Wales – the Miners' Welfare, the NCB, Glamorgan Education Authority, the BBC, etc. – would do no harm. After all, people with money usually take care of it and are loath to part with it. How do you write to millionaires? Are there any in Wales? I did not know. What if Gareth did not make the grade? That was ridiculous. He would make it all right. I was in fact looking for a sponsor, a practice unheard of in our area in those days.

The next time I spoke to Gareth it was in earnest. I told him of my plans. 'There are reasons why I think you should go. You need a platform in an established rugby school to show your talents. You will certainly get a Welsh Senior Schoolboy cap. You need an opportunity to develop your potential. You should represent the English Schools in hurdling. You can consolidate your 'O' levels and gain admission to do PE at Cardiff.'

While I was speaking, I could see that he was flabbergasted at my suggestion. 'I want you to promise me that you will do your best, and that you will never let anybody down.'

'Don't worry, Mr Samuel.'

'Tell your parents I'll see them tonight.'

As always it was cosy in the Edwards household. My meeting with them was going to be a difficult and sensitive one; money matters usually are. I informed them both of the developments which in the end meant that they would have to pay half the fees.

'That's impossible,' said Glan. 'We can't afford that; we'd be in debt for the rest of our lives.'

I had to agree with this. Miners earned very poor wages in those days.

'Mr Meyer wants me to try to get some money from the monied people. If I succeed, are you prepared to make some financial sacrifices on his behalf?'

Quite naturally they were apprehensive, but they agreed to allow me to negotiate for terms which would be acceptable to both parties. That night I could not sleep. I was composing letters.

'Dear Sir,

I would like to draw your attention to the extraordinary sporting talent of . . .'

How would they be received? It did not take long before I found out. One millionaire was often in the news in Wales, especially with his benevolence towards churches and chapels. I was, therefore, quite hopeful that he would respond kindly to my plea. Alas, it did not materialise in that way. He was prepared to support the sons and daughters of clerics, but not the sons of those outside the cloth. I wrote to another, only to discover that he did not support individuals, only charities. With two major setbacks my spirits sank to rock-bottom, but I did not give in. I wrote to every conceivable business – but all responded in the same negative vein. I then focused my attention on local businessmen.

'You can't make a silk purse out of a sow's ear,' one said to me (his son was in a small Welsh public school).

'Miner's boy in Millfield. What a laugh!' remarked another.

In my quest I had arranged to meet many people, far and wide, only to be rejected by each one in turn. One night, in particular, will live forever in my memory. There was a self-made man who had, by honest endeavours, become really rich. He was a passionate Welshman who believed that Welshmen, especially Welsh-speaking ones, were the salt of the earth. When I telephoned him, he agreed to meet me on 'a financial matter which, in my opinion, would be near his heart'.

We talked about things in general in his comfortable sitting-room, before he started speaking on the plight of Wales and of his disappointment with her. It did not take me long to realise that he was presenting a new philosophy to me about Wales. He warmed to his subject.

'Wales is governed by inadequate politicians and academics. Their ideas are so entrenched and outdated that any progress that is made

111

is stifled by their presence. Our best brains are given an academic education, and end up in England, to fill *their* schools with teachers, *their* hospitals with doctors, *their* courts with lawyers. This regular exodus of our best brains in the last seventy years has unquestionably denuded Wales of its richest talent and yet the system continues unhindered. Every year you see a group photograph of sixth formers, with the headmaster, of course, from local schools on their way, marked 'export', to Oxford or Cambridge Universities. What would happen to Wales if these very clever youngsters were given the opportunity of training in commerce and industry here in Wales? A legacy has prevailed which has inevitably implied, because miners and steelworkers were dirty-faced workers, that to work in any form of industry was undesirable and a clear indication of failure. The educational system was geared to stress the importance of the academic professions, to prop up the Establishment with a never-ending supply of brainwashed graduates whose blinkered education is of minimal value to the economy and development of Wales.'

He paused for a break, and to light another cigarette. Puffing away in a cloud of smoke, he continued, 'The Welsh nation is being welshed every day. I don't like that term,' he said, as an afterthought. 'Some Welsh Labour MPs taking off their caps after passing the Severn Tunnel, to live the life of an aristocrat in Westminster at the expense of the Welsh people.'

As I listened to this man I realised that I had landed in a hornet's nest. I was afraid to open my mouth because I was not quite sure whether he would relish what I had to propose to him. He went on and on. 'Welsh children are being suppressed and are prevented from being inventive and from developing their talents to make Wales into the promised land which it could very well be, but for the pot-bound system of education which is in existence.'

I tried to intervene politely, but this time his tirade was matched by the sheer anger on his face.

'It's the same with Welsh rugby,' I said.

Most Welshmen will fall for this bait, and he was no exception. 'Rugby in Wales, ever since I've known it, has been a hit-or-miss affair. We need players with flair.'

He had mentioned the word 'flair' and that gave me immediate confidence that he would be sympathetic to my plea.

'I know of such a boy. That is why I am here tonight. We have in Gwaun-cae-gurwen a miner's boy who has been offered a place in a rugby-playing public school in England providing I can get some financial support for him. It would prove a wonderful chance for the boy. He is Welsh-speaking and lives in a council house and needs help.'

As I was speaking I could see the impatience on my companion's face change to anger, and then I suffered one of the most humiliating experiences of my life. 'It is typical of small-minded men like you to do that. What is wrong in being Welsh-speaking, living in a council house and attending a local grammar school?'

This was a contradiction to what he had said previously. 'What is so grand in entering a public school in order to change one's identity? Why should a miner's son be something special in another environment? Why can't he be special in his own country?'

'But in a public school the facilities are better and the fixture list is more attractive,' I intervened.

'Too many times in the past I have seen brilliant young men go from their humble communities to raise their social standards to become middle-class and, much the pity, to have no time for their parents, their friends, their community and their country. No time even for some to return to their parents' funerals.'

'Gareth won't be like that. He's too level-headed. It's quite clear that you are not prepared to help him,' I said, beginning to lose my patience.

'My advice to you is, leave the boy where he is happiest and that is at Gwaun-cae-gurwen. *How Green Was My Valley* and *The Corn Is Green* express the tragedy of Wales. To think that the only worthwhile reward for a miner's son is in England, and not amongst his own people in Wales! If he becomes famous, there will be rich people with gold purses, waiting to lure him so that they can reflect in his glory. He won't want to know you because you are symbolic of his earlier days, when he was on the bottom rung of the social scale.'

I left his house with my tail firmly between my legs. His words were echoing in my ears as I drove homewards. I felt like a little boy who had been caught stealing and had received a good whipping. Some of those words had hurt me, and I had certainly got the message. What the hell! Why should I put myself in such a position? Would Gareth really turn out to be like that? Blow it! I'd wait until tomorrow, and inform him that the idea of Millfield had failed through lack of financial support.

That night Velda and I stayed up late, chatting, so that I could unwind. She was very sympathetic as I angrily related my experiences with the Welshman wise to the ways of money. He had whipped me and stirred my conscience and that was it, Gareth would stay in Wales. 'Sleep on it, Bill,' Velda said. 'You'll feel differently in the morning.' I looked at her in amazement and went to bed.

I wrote to Mr Meyer the following day, informing him of my disappointment in being unable to procure financial support for Gareth. I received assurances from him, by return of post, that he would endeavour to find a sponsor. He also suggested a date for us to visit Millfield.

In company with Gareth, sister Gloria and brother-in-law Clive, we made our first journey to the small village of Street in Somerset. As we came near to our destination, I realised that our conversation throughout our journey had been in Welsh. I urgently reminded Gareth that when we got to the school it would be common courtesy to speak only in English.

The school was not as opulent as I had expected. The classrooms were ex-army huts which were dispersed around the stately Millfield House. As befitted a headmaster well known for his cricketing prowess, the school was extraordinarily well blessed with facilities for that game. Mr Meyer turned out to be a tall, distinguished, good-looking middle-aged man, who greeted us warmly. As we walked around the school, Gareth became tongue-tied. When he did speak it was invariably in Welsh, which I translated. He was completely overawed by the situation. I felt I had to apologise, 'I am sorry that Gareth and I speak to each other in Welsh; we cannot help it, really, because it is our natural language. From now on both of us will make an effort, won't we, Gareth?'

'Don't worry one bit,' he said. 'We teach sixty-four languages here, and Welsh is one of them. I am glad to hear that it is alive and kicking. Carry on. I am enjoying it.'

His reaction impressed me, and so did his philosophy when he said, 'The British Empire has gone to the dogs. We must seek excellence in our brilliant young people to be assured of future glory. That is why I am keen on helping your young man.' We got along splendidly and in private conversation we discussed the question of fees.

'I must be honest: I am here to safeguard the financial interests of Mr and Mrs Edwards. I am not prepared to encourage them to go into debt,' I said quite frankly.

'The boy *must* come to Millfield. I am impressed with him.'

'Well, I'm sorry, there is no one in Wales prepared to help him,' I said sadly.

'Leave the matter with me. In the meantime, try to find out what the Edwardses can afford.'

We shook hands, bade farewell and journeyed homewards. Gareth was in a state of great exhilaration as he talked endlessly about the day's happenings. I was occupied in wrestling with financial problems as I pretended to be asleep. By the end of the journey I had arrived at a formula which I thought was fair and reasonable for the Edwardses to pay. It transpired that both supported me to the hilt, even though it would entail financial sacrifices on their part.

'We have great faith in you, Mr Samuel. You do what you think is right for Gareth,' said Glan with calm assurance.

Although both were supportive of my idea, I still wonder if they had moments of regret during Gareth's days at Millfield, for Mrs Edwards sewed into the small hours as a dressmaker, whilst Glan had to drive buses in his spare time.

In August I received a letter from Mr Meyer. 'Let him come if you are all keen.' The message still rings with the same excitement now as it did then, over twenty years ago. All my worries vanished with the glad tidings. My plans were about to be realised. Gareth would have his stage after all.

'It is only because I got a little help from an Englishman whose grandmother was Welsh that I can help to finance Gareth for a year, which ought to be two. Your own enthusiasm, of course, has done even more to bring me to my decision,' wrote Jack Meyer after what seemed to me to be years of negotiation. Gareth was speechless when he saw the letter and realised the gist of its contents.

'It's great, Mr Samuel! How can I ever thank you for what you've done for me?'

'My reward will be your success. The door is ajar. As you go through it, make sure that on your return your head will go through it as well.'

'Oh, I won't be like that. That's for sure.'

'Many men have forfeited their principles at the rustle of a few fivers.' I realised I was lecturing again. 'By Christmas you'll be speaking with a tight upper lip, like an Oxford don. You will want to forget the language of the Waun collier.' He laughed loudly at the notion.

'That's one thing I'll never do,' he said, with natural conviction.

When I went back to school in September it was a strange experience not to find him there. He had provided me with expectation, excitement and success for the last three years. I was not despondent at his departure, though; there would be plenty of boys with spark to come in his wake. Perhaps there could be one better?

I remember Mr Thomas, the headmaster, mentioning in the school assembly one morning that he had received a letter from Millfield in which Gareth had conveyed his thanks to the staff for helping him along the way. Mr Thomas enjoyed the tribute. He made the staff and children laugh when he mentioned that 'Mr Samuel not only taught him PT and scripture, but he looked after his body and soul'.

Gareth was seventeen when he went to Millfield. Mr Sid Hill, the biology master, who hailed from Morriston in the Swansea Valley, was the master in charge of rugby there. He was a former Swansea University player. Sid was of the opinion that Gareth could make a better contribution to the team by playing as a full-back. He was not wrong in thinking of alternative positions for him to play, for he was good enough to play for Wales in any position. It did not take long for Sid to discover that the nearer Gareth was to the ball, the more dangerous he became. He was extraordinarily gifted as a goal-kicker and broke the school's goal-kicking record. He would have done so at international level too, but for his easy-going manner. How Wales could have benefited from his kicking, especially in the matches against New Zealand at the Arms Park! Both games could have been won by consistent kicking.

When Gareth had been interviewed for entry into Millfield he had been told that it would be expected of him to be tolerant of young people with different talents. They were to help each other in learning different skills whether they were artistic, scientific or sporting. I was somewhat amused when Gareth informed me that he had been testing and measuring in PE and that many of his new friends were doing schedules on circuit, target and weight training. That was over twenty years ago. It was only recently that the WRU became aware that such systems existed.

In those days Millfield did not play inter-school rugby in the second term; they concentrated on sevens at the end of the spring term. All schools who play sevens to a high level gather at the prestigious Roehampton schoolboy seven-a-side tournament in March. In 1965, Millfield, in brilliant style, emerged winners and Gareth was deemed the best player of the tournament. John Reason of the *Daily Telegraph* earmarked him as the next golden boy of Welsh rugby, which was a credit to John's ability to pick talent. Gareth was also selected, without much resistance, to play for the Welsh Secondary Schools.

As soon as it became known that I was responsible for getting Gareth into Millfield I found that people who had always considered themselves superior were condescending to speak to me in the hope that I would support them to get their boys into the school at cut-price rates. 'How can I get my son to Millfield?' 'My son is a better prospect than Edwards.' 'I'll give you £5 a lesson [remember, this was 1964] if you take my son under your wing.'

It became a nauseating experience when they came in luxurious cars, pleading poverty, wanting me to work miracles to get their sons in on the cheap. I helped two young men the following year because both of them, Nick Williams, New Quay, and Wayne Lewis, Llandybie, were outstanding schoolboy athletes and rugby players, but, more importantly, they were impeccably behaved.

Gareth was encouraged by Mr Meyer to stay on for an extra year. Mr and Mrs Edwards unhesitatingly supported the idea, which was a brave and unselfish thing to do; the fees remained a formidable amount to pay.

When he came home for the Easter holidays in 1966, it had crossed my mind that he could be invited to play for one of the local first-class clubs. In my experience, too many young stars had been tempted to play for first-class teams when they were too immature, with the result that many had fallen by the wayside, victims of their own inexperience.

Many selectors can remember players playing badly, but only a few can recall their better games. I was therefore alert to the fact that a first-class club might entice Gareth to play without my knowing anything at all about it. It was a crucial period in his playing career and it could be spoilt by one hasty attempt to please an unscrupulous rugby club.

My premonition was proved right, for the *Western Mail* disclosed that the Millfield star had been selected to play for a famous first-class club that Friday evening. I was annoyed; the disclosure could have been based on one of two facts: Gareth consenting to play, or being selected without being asked – an old ploy which was familiar to me. Not many young players could refuse an open invitation of that nature to play for a famous club, especially when their name appeared in Wales's national paper. Gareth fell for the bait. We were having tea at home that evening when Glan Edwards walked in, obviously dressed for the occasion.

'Are you coming?' he asked, looking pleased with himself.

'Where to?' I asked, pretending not to know about the selection.

'Why, haven't you seen it in the *Western Mail*? He's been picked to play for . . . tonight. He wants you to come. I've got the car outside. He's waiting at home with his kit ready,' he said with great excitement.

'Did they ask him to play?' I asked calmly.

'No, but it's in the *Western Mail*!'

'If he does play tonight, tell him it's the end of our partnership.'

Glan's face fell. He had clearly not expected such a negative reaction.

'But it's a great chance, a wonderful chance. To think they've picked him without seeing him play.'

'That's an old trick of theirs. If he plays tonight, that's the end. The cheek of it – without even asking! *We* are the ones who will decide which club he'll play for – no club will dictate to us what to do.'

Glan left, quite deflated.

That night my ears did not stop tingling. Gareth must have been in an irate mood. I was sure he would not play. The following morning's *Western Mail* verified my confidence.

In his final term at Millfield he became the British schoolboy champion in the hurdles, breaking the record in the attempt, and also beating the eventual great English Olympic hurdler Alan Pascoe in the process.

When Gareth finished at Millfield, Mr Meyer wrote to me, 'Gareth, alas, has moved on, the better I hope for his days at Millfield. I doubt if I shall see his like again, for of all the top-class performers in various fields of school activity, he was on his own.'

By this time I was confident that Gareth would emerge as the best Welsh scrum-half of all time and I expressed these thoughts to a young neighbour, Hywel Morgan, a former captain of the University of Wales XV. However, the astonishment on his face at hearing such predictions suddenly made me realise that it was unwise to sing the young player's praises too strongly in public. I soon discovered, much to my disappointment, that not all people were delighted with his sudden eminence. Jealousy and envy are unpleasant characteristics of human nature, and they were soon evident in the condemnation of the emerging young star. To my even greater disappointment and surprise, two WRU national coaches were not impressed with him.

When I saw the young Mervyn Davies play for London Welsh for the first time at Llanelli, I was completely captivated by his contribution to the game. In conversation after the game with a famous coach, I asked him to name a London Welsh forward who, on the day's performance, was destined to play for Wales. He named three forwards, and Mervyn was not one of them. This convinced me further that there were many conspicuous men at high level in Welsh rugby who could not recognise a great player when they saw one.

Gareth's next step was to fulfil his ambition of becoming a physical education teacher, a job for which he was eminently suitable, for he adored children. He opted to do his training at the Cardiff College of Education, and so it was logical that the Cardiff Rugby Club should be the club of his choice. Llanelli was the more natural club choice, for Gareth was Welsh-speaking and I, too, had a strong connection with the club, having played rugby with most of its committee members. Swansea was also a temptation, but they already possessed a scrum-half who promised a great future, so that gateway was closed and I received no encouragement to induce him to play for the famous Whites. I had known both secretaries, Ken Jones of Llanelli and David Price of Swansea, personally for years, and both had the human ingredients necessary to guide a young player along the right path, but finally the overriding factor was that Gareth was going to be educated at Cardiff.

Once again Cardiff were going to benefit from the talents of West Wales rugby players – although they were unaware of it as yet.

Chapter Nine

Shared Achievement

That summer Gareth and I were busily preparing for the Cardiff RFC trials. Everything was going well until he pulled a leg muscle, which caused us so much anxiety that he was forced to go to his doctor, Dr Seth Jones. Some time later the doctor told me, 'I've never come across such a tough young man. I had so much difficulty injecting him that I broke two needles in the attempt.'

He recovered from that setback and renewed his commitment to training. It was a strange experience for both of us. We met regularly and imagined we were playing on the Arms Park and not on Parc-y-Werin, Gwaun-cae-gurwen. 'Don't you think that I should start by playing for Cwmgors?' he asked me one evening during a spell in training.

'Playing for your village team is an important step for those not possessed of all the skills. You have all the skills already; you only need two things – the opportunity to show what you can do, and time to gain experience. You don't start at the bottom, because you are already superior to what is at the top.'

'Do you really believe that?' he asked incredulously.

'You are going to be surprised. Pillars in the rugby world, who know very little about player-assessment, will be puzzled by your standard of play. They'll want confirmation and assurance that you're not a one-season wonder. There will be those jealous and reluctant to give you praise, and there will be many who will find fault.'

'If it's going to be like that, it won't be worth it, will it?'

'Of course it will be worth it. You cannot hope to get all people on your side, especially the Welsh. The best rugby player Wales ever had, according to the Llanelli supporters, was Albert Jenkins, who played in the '20s, and the best half-backs, according to the Swansea supporters, were the James brothers. This is the beauty about Welsh support; it is fervently parochial to the point of absurdity. There are Under-Fifteen schoolboy packs today far bigger than the legendary Welsh Terrible Eight of the latter period of the last century. You will have to convince people entrenched in out-of-date ideas that you are a symbol of the new approach to rugby, and that is why we are preparing now, while the unsuspecting are asleep, you may say, for the first of your many visits to the Cardiff Arms Park.'

He would smile at my orations and fantasies, half believing my sincerity. I would laugh at his reactions and, out of relief more than anything else, he would join in heartily. 'You're pulling my leg. I don't know whether you're serious or not.'

Later on in the summer I wrote a letter to the Cardiff club, asking them to consider including Gareth in one of their preliminary trials. I could not help stating in the letter that he was the best prospect I had ever seen. Within a few days a circular answer came through the post without any words of encouragement.

I had made sure that he was fitter than at any time in his subsequent career. Any young player wishing to make an impression needs to be fitter at the beginning of the season than the established player, because the older, more established player may not have bothered to seek peak fitness at the time. When we got to the Arms Park I noticed that things had changed considerably from the days I was there in 1952–53; the members attending the trial had diminished significantly. I was greeted warmly by the chairman, Mr Gwyn Porter, a fine sportsman who had served the club well as a player and committee man. It dawned on me instantly that he was not particularly struck with my companion, and the reason for that, I thought, was that the club already possessed two brilliant West-Walian scrum-halfs in Billy Hullin, the club captain, and Gary Samuel, an international in ability, who was never fully recognised in Wales.

In a condescending tone, Gwyn told me, 'The committee have decided to play your boy in the second half.'

'Second half! Surely you can't be serious, Gwyn? This boy's dynamite,' I replied, controlling my anger.

'We get dozens of letters every year from well-meaning people recommending world-beaters, but the majority prove to be useless,' Gwyn replied, rather superciliously.

'It's not my nature to bring nincompoops to Cardiff. You are wrong about this one. He should play a full game,' I said with conviction, as I walked dejectedly away.

It was quite evident from my conversation with Gwyn that the Cardiff club were more than content with their top-class scrum-halfs. To bring in another would only complicate matters.

Gareth was completely overawed by the situation – a dream come true. When I informed him that he was to play only in the second half, he lifted my spirits by saying, 'I'm lucky to be playing at all, with such famous players standing around.' On the way I had outlined a plan of campaign for the two halves. I scrapped that one and evolved a new one.

'This is your big day, Gareth. Show them that you can pass, kick, tackle and run. Harass your opponent. Suggest to the captain that you can kick goals.' As I was speaking, I could see the seriousness in his face. 'You get changed into your tracksuit. Warm up twenty minutes before half-time, and then come and see me for the final briefing.'

The trial was held at Sophia Gardens and, as expected, I met many an old friend who was curious at my presence, but I refrained from exposing my association with one of the trialists.

Just before half-time, there was Gareth before me, perspiring profusely. 'How are you feeling? Not scared, are you?' I asked with a smile. He replied, with a broad grin, 'I'm not scared, but I *am* nervous.'

'Well done! All great performers are nervous before they go on the stage,' I said encouragingly. 'This is the plan. When are the opposing wing forwards least effective?'

'Midfield, around the halfway mark.'

'Good! Wait for a scrum around that area if possible. If it's your put-in, you should win the strike. Pick up the ball and, as quick as a flash, run towards the opposing outside-half, sell him a dummy, side-step the full-back and score under the posts, OK?' I didn't realise the matter-of-fact way in which I was speaking.

'All right,' he said, with a grin on his face. This was a challenge, just between him and me. I had no doubt at all whether he could accomplish the task; I was positive he could, for I was certain he had the skill, determination and speed to do it.

The Cardiff Rugby Club had adopted a very sensible method of invigilating their trial games. They dispersed their committee members at various locations around the pitch so that all the trialists were under close observation all the time.

I took his tracksuit and training shoes from him and, finally, said to him, 'Show these city types what the Welsh-speaking peasants of the Swansea Valley can do.' With that he went on to the field.

Scrum-halfs cannot help but be in the picture straight away, but Gareth appeared quite harmless, fulfilling his role efficiently as a member of his team. When the opponents knocked on at the halfway line and a scrum was formed, I could feel my pulse increasing its tempo. It was zero-hour.

Time to blow the fuse! Without showing any indication at all of going on his own, he executed the ploy with so much ease that one might have imagined the defending players changed into blocks of wood. The few spectators in attendance gave him rousing applause. 'Scora un arall! Score another one!' I shouted to him in Welsh. One cannot seriously expect a boy to listen to that type of request, but in his case it was just a matter of calling the number, such was his confidence and relationship with me. Even when the defence had been alerted, he still managed to score another try. That time there was a jink and a kick ahead on his way to the goal-line.

When the trial ended, some of the trialists realised that they had played in the company of a potential rugby genius and went to shake his hand. The committee members also appreciated the fact that they had witnessed an extraordinary young player, and converged on him from their various posts to shake the hand of a very shy young man. A beaming Gwyn Porter, whose attitude had changed by now, was insistent that the Cardiff club would welcome him with open arms. The genial character Stan Bowes, a pillar of the Cardiff club who is well known in the rugby world, came up to me and said, 'He promises to be the best West Walian ever' – which, coming from a stout Cardiffian like Stan, was indeed a compliment!

When Gareth went to college, I accepted the fact that our partnership was about to be broken up. The young fledgling was about to fly away from its nest and seek its independence. Some people have maintained that I should have stuck to him like glue, to share his prominence, to be by his side whenever and wherever he played. To reflect in his undoubted brilliance. To meet the affluent and the influential, and to shake hands and keep company with the famous. Most of all, to project myself and seek favours so that I would improve myself, as others had done before, in the social circle. The way towards my own personal advancement and possibly that of my young family was open if I continued my close relationship with Gareth. That was the advice proffered by many.

Rightly or wrongly, I was not made that way. I had no mercenary claims at all. There was no financial reward which could replace the happiness that I had derived from developing a small boy to become the most talked-about Welsh rugby player of all time. I had exhausted my knowledge of teaching for him to become a super-player. There was nothing else to teach him and at nineteen, in most cases, he would not receive any further individual teaching from first-class clubs, only team coaching. He was equipped both physically and mentally for the big time, and my share of his glory would only be in a job well done. There would be others, with more guile than I, ready to exploit him in various ways. It had happened before, and it would happen again. 'Stick close to him, Bill,' said one wise man to me. 'If you want to go on a free Lions tour, there are plenty of benefactors around with silk purses who would be prepared to pay for your trip as long as you are ready to keep them close to Gareth. There are people with apartments and villas in Spain and Portugal who would gladly provide you with a holiday, just because of your connection.'

Those were incredible statements to make to someone like me in 1970. I was completely unaware that wealthy people existed in Wales who would engage in such transactions. As I followed Gareth's career from a distance, however, it became obvious to me that the wise man's assertions of 1970 were blatantly true; there *were* such people around.

We all have our basic principles, or moral codes. Mine were acquired at home and in the community, where we were taught that the best service was given by unseen hands. I never so much as gave Gareth the chance to buy me a glass of beer.

When Gareth appeared on the Welsh rugby scene for the first time, his reception was too good to be true. He was receiving compliments from all quarters. From my experience of the Welsh people's tendency to find fault, I knew the day was not distant when they would find blemishes in his playing (and, if they did not exist, they would soon invent them!).

I decided to watch Cardiff's next home game and, if the opportunity arose, to confer with my old friend, Bleddyn Williams, whose opinion I valued highly. After the match, in which Gareth had given a good account of himself, I went to the Athletic Club and there, true to form, was Bleddyn, with his brother Lloyd, with whom I had also had the honour of playing when he was a youngster with the club. Bleddyn was, as he is now, the rugby correspondent of the *Sunday People*. He had his finger on the pulse of Welsh rugby. He had access to all the rumours and speculations about rugby. What was his assessment of Gareth? Lloyd's remarks would be interesting.

One could not help but admire the Williams brothers: not only had they been superlative players, they also possessed a comprehensive knowledge of the game. In addition, they were honest people who would rather offend than tell a lie.

'Your young man caused a bit of a stir in this game tonight, Bill,' commented Bleddyn.

'He's an exciting prospect, I must confess,' I replied.

'Lloyd and I have agreed that there is something extra special about him, haven't we Lloyd?'

'The only doubt I have is that, although his passing is adequate, he needs to gain extra speed on his flick-passes,' Lloyd stated.

'You are quite right,' I said. 'He's only nineteen. Give him a year and his passing, like his line-kicking, will, I have no doubt, improve.'

'How do you rate him?' asked Bleddyn, putting me on the spot.

'I suppose, with due grace and modesty, I should say wait and see, but since I have a great deal of respect for both of you, I am positively sure he's going to be the best you've ever seen,' I said confidently. They both paused, then Bleddyn spoke once again.

'That's one hell of a big claim to make, Bill, but if it's any consolation to you, Lloyd and I have already made up our minds, and we are inclined to agree with your prophecy. Let's hope for the sake of Wales that we can again reach the heights, with your young man leading the way.'

Such a compliment coming from that source was indeed a tonic.

Wales, as a rugby nation, was at that time in a definite state of crisis. The Welsh supporters were in the doldrums. The standard of play was at its lowest ebb in years. The sense of dedication from the players had gone. Coaching, instituted in 1967, was considered to be the panacea for the Welsh Rugby Union troubles, but, in 1968, some people were expecting too much too soon from the coaching system.

When it was announced that Gareth had been selected for the Welsh team and won his first cap, I felt no excitement, since his selection was, as far as I was concerned, inevitable. When I phoned him to extend my congratulations, he too had accepted his honour in a low key. There was jubilation and celebration at the college and similarly in Gwaun-cae-gurwen. There was one thing for sure: he was not going to be a one-cap wonder. Many people asked me, 'Are you going to France, Bill?' They were amazed when I told them I was not. I had made up my mind that I was not prepared to spend money I could ill afford on my own pleasure. The money I had in the bank was not much, but it was enough as a stand-by, in case of emergencies, as the welfare of my four young children was uppermost in my mind. However, that personal resolution was not finally adhered to, for Mr and Mrs Edwards came to see me a few days before the match. They sat down, had coffee and chatted quite happily about the forthcoming event. We speculated about the prospects for the match, then the inevitable question was posed. 'Are *you* going to Paris, Mr Samuel?'

I had anticipated the question and dreaded replying to it. 'No, I have decided not to go because, since Gareth is a scrum-half, I will see more of him on TV than I would in the packed Stade Colombes.'

'Glan and I think you should go,' replied Mrs Edwards firmly. 'You must go. It's not only Gareth's achievement, but yours as well. Without you, he would never have been selected for Wales.'

I felt myself blushing as I realised what she was saying. I felt ashamed that I had not already booked my ticket to Paris. It was my *duty* to go and support Gareth, and to be proud of him and not make excuses.

As soon as she had finished speaking she opened her bag and produced a small roll of one-pound notes held together by an elastic band. She handed it to me. 'There is an excursion going to Paris on Friday evening for twelve pounds,' said Glan. 'We realise you can't afford it, with four young children and Velda not working. It's only a small payment, but we have decided you must be the first to go.'

'But you must find your own pocket-money!' Mrs Edwards exclaimed triumphantly. I was completely overwhelmed by their kindness. Twelve pounds was equivalent to a fortnight's pay for them at that time. I made a feeble effort to return the money, but they were adamant. When they left, much later, Velda and I returned to the house.

'Surely you don't intend keeping the money those lovely people gave you?' asked Velda.

'I have no intention of keeping it,' I answered truthfully, 'but you saw how determined they were to give some form of acknowledgement.'

'Take it back, take it back now or I won't be able to sleep tonight. Go to France like everyone else. We'll find the money from somewhere.' Without hesitation I jumped into my Mini with the twelve pounds secure in my pocket. The Edwardses objected, of course, but their protests went unheeded. I realised that I had made them happy and that I could go to Paris with a clear conscience. I felt a warm glow when I realised that the Edwardses really appreciated my association with Gareth. They were the only ones who knew all the story.

Later on in the week I found a place on a charter flight from Cardiff for twenty-three pounds fifty. I withdrew fifty pounds from the bank and joined a delirious group of rugby supporters from the nearby village of Brynaman, whose company proved a tonic in itself. Gareth played an adequate game in France, just enough without taking any risks to ensure that he was in the Welsh team to play England at the Arms Park; to realise his biggest ambition and his fondest dream.

That game was long remembered as the day of another Welsh golden boy, Keith Jarrett, who set the place alight with a magnificent display of points-scoring. It was also a notable day in that it was David Watkins's last game before turning professional and Dewi Bebb announced that he was retiring after playing thirty-four games for Wales.

During the course of the game, Gareth made two blatant errors due to a lack of concentration. I was curious to discover how he would react to his lapses. He had been nurtured on the understanding that every game he played in my presence would be analysed by me. We would not be concerned with the things he could accomplish perfectly, but with aspects of his game that failed to reach performance standard. In the match against England he had committed two major errors which were not pinpointed by any professional observer. Gareth was aware that he had made two mistakes that day which were potentially dangerous; if England had snapped up the errors, they could have scored. When I saw him later he said with a big smile, 'Don't tell me, I know! I kicked the ball from a scrum near the touchline to the open field, and if the English wing had caught it, he would have scored. And the second error was passing the ball from a lineout with my back towards the opposing wing forward. He nearly intercepted, didn't he?' I looked at him with a great deal of pride and realised that his self-analysis was an indication to me that Jack now knew as much as his master and that it was now an opportune moment for me to retreat from the scene and allow him his liberty. My work was complete.

This was the time when Gareth's passing received some stick. The reporters had to invent a vulnerable aspect of his game in order to create some doubt and discussion. Even the inexpert were deriding him and succeeded in making him believe that he was vulnerable in this respect. The irony was that many of his sternest critics had never produced scrum-halfs of quality when *they* were teachers and coaches. I have taught many scrum-halfs who have played at all levels. Scrum-halfs are a special breed, but they do require one particular skill – the ability to pass.

Gareth never had any difficulty in finding his man. He would practise with a leather rugby ball filled with sand to develop distance. He used a car tyre attached by a rope to a hook in the ceiling to create a pendulum through whose centre he would pass the ball as it moved to and fro. He was pressure-trained for reflex action. Whoever instigated the rumour about a chink in his armour, however, managed to unnerve him and caused him to lose his confidence. Passing, like kicking, takes years of practice. It also takes two to make a pass. Barry's alignment in set positions did not suit Gareth, especially in defensive situations in their first game together. Barry had conditioned himself to run backwards before he kicked the ball from a set lineout or scrum position in a defensive role. It was the perfect way to keep the wing forward at a distance. With the Edwards pass there was no need to continue with that method, for he was given enough space and time to go forward to kick the ball into touch. I mentioned the weakness to Gareth at the time, and since both were extremely intelligent rugby players, the error was corrected. As Barry said in his very interesting book, 'And with Gareth's long pass, the best in the world, I had even more time.'

Prior to this development, outside-halfs had been hounded into error by quick breakaways from loose forwards. With the Edwards pass, they were given space and splendid isolation, a luxury never before given to them. Those who remain critical of his passing can observe the evidence of his early passing ability by watching TV replays of his early matches for Wales. His mastery of every type of pass was unparalleled in the history of Welsh rugby.

Another example of his aptitude, determination and ability to improvise was revealed when the dispensation law came into being. His kicking into touch at this point was impeccable. With the needs of the new law, he set about working on his bounce-kicking once again, which eventually resulted in his gaining 75 yards for his team at times. These were, indeed, breathtaking moments.

One physical endowment in which he was fortunate was his low centre of gravity. His hurdling had developed his ability to run in the bent position – essential for the position of scrum-half, especially when it is coupled with an uncanny strength and determination such as Gareth possessed. He could lift a bar with a weight of 230lbs (slightly more than sixteen stone) over his head when he was sixteen. No wonder, therefore, that the Welsh crowds were expecting him to go on his own from five yards out.

'When are you going to score a try from long distance in an international match?'

'Bill, you don't understand. Things are tough out there.'

'If you want to be remembered as an extraordinary scrum-half, you must attempt the unexpected and not just the predictable.'

'The opportunities do not arise as often as they did in school.'

'Human nature is the same all over the world. Wing forwards tend to relax in situations where they do not expect a scrum-half break. Eighty yards out is where you should alert yourself for such a try.'

Gareth laughed at the idea. 'You never give in, do you Bill? You want me to be a *Boys' Own* hero.'

'You have untapped reserves which need to be exploited. Remember those steps leading up to the golf club at Pontardawe? What about the times you raced over those 200 yards hurdles? You've completed thousands of weight, target and circuit training exercises. What about those press-ups with David John standing on your back? Running a hundred yards on the Arms Park in front of sixty-two thousand people should be just up your street. Surely you're not going to forfeit all that training to be recognised in years to come as just another scrum-half?'

As I was speaking to him I observed that every word was sinking in. 'All right,' he said, 'I'll bear it in mind this season.'

From that conversation ensued his try against Scotland, an unforgettable twelve seconds of speed, power, physical skill and sheer determination. It was acclaimed as the zenith of his achievements and, according to the critics, it was considered to be the best individual international try of all time.

I was particularly interested in the 1971 Lions tour of New Zealand and in their reaction to Gareth Edwards. He never received unanimous praise from their media, yet in the third Test he had a hand in the three tries scored. He was never given full credit for his contribution to that vital Test. Was there a prevailing hostility in New Zealand against a foreign scrum-half? No one could doubt the quality of Sid Going, the New Zealand scrum-half; he was a brilliant player who ignored convention and was a law unto himself on the field of play. His immediate predecessor, Chris Laidlaw, was another player of considerable merit. Was Gareth a threat to New Zealand's superiority in this position? Both New Zealand scrum-halfs had the advantage of playing regularly behind excellent packs. What would have happened if Gareth had had such protection throughout his playing career?

Thus I speculated and consequently was upset when, some months after the tour, a famous rugby journalist asked me whether Gareth 'lacked guts'. From what he said, a certain 'authority' had expressed his opinion that Gareth would 'chicken out' in a crisis. Thankfully Gareth's courage was never in doubt, but it shows how damaging and unkind people can be.

If New Zealanders were somewhat reticent in praising Gareth, other countries did not support their view. In the 1972 *Rothman's Rugby Union Yearbook*, the editor had asked eight of the world's best rugby critics to choose a World XV. For the scrum-half position Gareth received six votes, Sid Going one (from the French critic) and Max Barran of France one (from New Zealand).

New Zealanders have been the most popular of all the rugby tourists in Wales. Throughout my lifetime I recall that the great Kiwi players of the past have been surrounded by an aura of folklore and legend. Whatever the environment – colliery, steelworks, staff room, public house – if the discussion was about rugby, there was always a certain awed respect for New Zealand rugby and its great players. When Gareth went there on tour in 1971, one of my dreams was fulfilled. The driving-force behind our training was, to a considerable degree, an urge to beat New Zealand, because to my mind they share with South Africa the distinction of being the best rugby-playing nation in the world. For a small country to take on the might of the rugby world as New Zealand has done for the last century and beat them with regularity is testimony to their character as a nation. New Zealand's population is slightly in excess of Wales's, but the souls of both countries were united in their love of the game. They respected each other – until recently, when unpleasant incidents marred what had been, to me and my generation, a magnificent friendship.

The New Zealand tour during the WRU's centenary year showed clearly how wide the difference in ability between Wales and New Zealand is now. The All Blacks were superior in every facet of play. We insist on playing a type of game which is completely out of date. At one time the Lions were the champions and Wales dominated the home championship, while New Zealand remained a 'bogey side'. But for some inexplicable reason we lost the initiative of that period. Instead of concentrating on producing players of a similar mould, the emphasis moved to coaching team methods – 'the methodology of rugby football' – like conducting an orchestra when the musicians cannot read music. The concentration on team skills instead of individual speed, skill, stamina and strength scuttled any hope of another golden era.

'I must say, no coach ever tried to put me into a straight jacket of his own ideas. I am an individualist and coaches let me have my own way,' said Barry John. If that was true of Barry, it was also true of Gerald Davies, J.P.R., Mervyn Davies, John Taylor, etc., for they were great individualists, equipped to play top-class rugby with any great team in the world. Barry's game was not shaped by a coaching book, but in the Gwendraeth Valley, where he developed a system of playing which was to endear him to fellow players and opponents alike.

I suppose it's quite easy to look back on the successes of 1971 and 1974. Glory is far more enjoyable than failure, as witnesses to Gareth's homecoming from the tours will readily verify. The streets of Gwaun-cae-gurwen were thronged with people in carnival spirits and the Welfare Hall was packed to capacity.

That was the last time I saw Gareth until late October of the 1972–73 season. I was not aware that there was a crisis in his rugby career until I met Barry John after a charity soccer match in Clydach. I had been enticed by my younger son, Iestyn, to go and watch that particular Sunday match, because the great Ivor Allchurch (Newcastle and Wales inside forward) had been included amongst other celebrities in the match. Just one more glimpse of the soccer genius before he retires, I said to myself. Ivor did not let us down; he scored with a glorious shot from thirty-five yards.

As the game was being played, Iestyn and I stood near the touchline, enjoying the play. When Barry John was involved nearby and had cleared the ball, he gave me a shout, 'I want to see you after the game.' Later, he came to us. 'It's a good thing you were here today or I would have phoned you,' he said, with concern.

'What's the matter?' I asked.

'It's Gareth. He seems to have lost the urge to play. He's a shadow of his former self. If he continues as he is now, he will definitely lose his place in the Cardiff team. You'd better see him, because he needs your help.'

My spirits dropped instantly.

'Oh, yes, he's lost interest, and is very lackadaisical in everything he does,' Barry continued.

What was the trouble? Had he lost his confidence because Barry had retired? Was the domestic scene a disappointment after the euphoria of victory over New Zealand? I rang him that evening. 'I understand that you're playing badly,' I said.

'Who told you that?' he asked, defensively.

'Never mind. He's a very close friend of yours and is so concerned that he has asked me to do something about it. If you can make it, I'll see you in the gym tomorrow morning at ten. Bring your kit with you. A school lunch won't do you any harm.'

I must be honest, I was unsure whether he would turn up. After all, he was a celebrity and I a mere teacher. I was as thrilled as the children when he walked into the gymnasium the following day. We chatted for a while.

'I'm fed up with rugby. I just can't be bothered to train,' he said, without much spirit.

'Too much rugby is like too much ice cream. It can be bad for you. Don't worry about it. Just follow the boys doing their exercises and see what happens.'

It was just the therapy he needed. He enjoyed being in the gym, and his sagging spirits began to disappear. During our rest periods, his mind was revitalised. At the end of the day he returned home-wards to Porthcawl visibly more contented than he had been on his arrival.

'Bring your rugby kit with you tomorrow as well. I've got an afternoon of rugby lessons. You'll enjoy that!'

He joined in with a session of basic skill training with a group of young boys. He was delighted with the involvement. Later on, the sixth formers came for their lesson, and suddenly he realised that rugby was a tough game once again, for he was not having his own way with members of the Cwmtawe First XV in the group. Their enthusiasm was passed on to him. British Lion or not, if he had the ball he was an instant target to be felled. When the session was over, he was tired.

'These boys know how to play rugby, Bill,' he said. 'They certainly know how to tackle.'

'They believe in the old adage "the bigger they are, the harder they fall" – whether they are big, or big stars, as in your case,' I said, with a smile.

'You don't change, do you Bill? You understand how I tick, and you're the only one I can trust to put my rugby right. I was beginning to lose my direction in the game. These two days with you have proved conclusively that I need to discipline myself. Don't you worry about me again. I won't let you down.'

'You have only written a few chapters of your book just yet; the best chapters are to come,' I assured him.

Once more he manned the headlines: 'Gareth shows New Zealand form'; 'Better than ever'. He never looked back after that and went on to win 53 consecutive caps for Wales.

Wales lost only once at the Arms Park in the Five Nations Championship during the time he played for them. He appeared in two successful Lions tours. He was at his best in his final four years for Wales, when they lost only twice and won three Championships, three Triple Crowns and two Grand Slams. He scored twenty tries. The WRU made him captain of Wales at the age of twenty, the youngest ever. It was a great honour, but I would not have burdened him with the captaincy. To shackle him with such a responsibility could only result in his playing below his instinctive best.

I saw his first game for Wales in Paris and his final match against France at the Arms Park. His final flourish was a drop-goal to help Wales win the Grand Slam.

There is no need for me to defend him now. The greatest players of the '70s singled him out from the galaxy of stars as the force which made the difference. It was universally felt that had he been present on the 1977 tour of New Zealand, the Lions would have won. Players of the calibre of Phil Bennett and Fran Cotton said it.

What is my reaction to his prodigious success? I consider myself very lucky. It was rugby and its players that changed the direction of my life. I wanted to be like them, and it was they who nudged me in the early days to seek a higher station in life. I did not achieve glory, but I could try to help others. In that attempt, I had the good fortune to teach many excellent schoolboys – but Gareth was, as they say, the icing on the cake.

Chapter Ten

Rugby Fever

It was great to be a Welsh rugby-supporter in the '70s. The Welsh XV possessed the ingredients to win most of their internationals against the home countries. The media were hard put to it to find new and adequate adjectives to do justice to rugby's rejuvenation. Certain players possessed charismatic qualities which endeared them to friend and foe alike. John Bevan, J.J. Williams and Gerald Davies, the wing three-quarters, epitomised the variety of entertainment which was provided. How was it that Wales produced such a crop of talented players at the same time? Was it a fluke? A freak situation? Or was it, as is claimed by the WRU, the result of their coaching system?

Out of chaos comes order, so they say. In this context, the chaos was the 1939–45 war. Participation in sport during the war became almost non-existent, but it did not prevent the young men in the armed forces and those who remained at the home front from pining for their lost opportunities and dreaming of the days when once again they would be free to engage in their favourite sports. When the hostilities ceased there was a great renaissance in sport in Great Britain. The football stadiums were packed with enthusiastic supporters and every available playing-field was utilised by players released from the shackles of war, anxiously making up for lost time.

Along with this sense of euphoria there arrived a new breed of physical educationists, who were anxious to place properly trained physical education teachers in our schools. Colleges such as Loughborough, Carnegie and St Luke's grew to be the pioneers in this field. These professionally trained men changed the course of physical education in our schools.

In the county of Glamorgan, for example, PE became a compulsory subject. It entailed two lessons in the gymnasium or school hall, and two lessons of games. This system proved its worth, because a county like Glamorgan produced an Olympic gold medallist (Lyn Davies) and an England cricket captain (Tony Lewis) – an incredible achievement. The best long jumper (on his day) in the world? A *Welshman* captaining the *England* XI? These triumphs belong to the world of fiction rather than that of fact. And then, in addition, there were several British Lions. The PE lessons were inspected regularly by county inspectors, Gordon and Brychan Davies and David Rees, to ensure that the work was done properly. One or two teachers resented being made accountable in that way, but I enjoyed it, for I felt that the system made me a better teacher.

This change was not confined to Glamorgan, coming into operation in the other counties of Wales as well. It was a dynamic infusion of expertise which resulted in renewed vigour and success in a subject which had lain fallow for many years. The standards of rugby, soccer, athletics and cricket began to change dramatically. All schools took part in physical education because they were instructed to compete and to enjoy the available sports. PE became a craze. Competitions in gymnastics, championships in athletics, school and district teams in soccer and rugby found a new prominence. Young men clamoured to qualify as PE masters, many of them members of the Welsh team of the '70s.

Many a boy attending these schools did not want to play, but because inter-school games had been arranged, they had no choice but to participate. What could one do when there were only a few boys wanting to play for the school?

'I don't want to play, sir.'

'What? Don't want to play the best game in the world?'

'I have never played before, sir.'

'Never mind, I'll teach you. With your size and speed, boy, you'll play the other pack on your own within a fortnight.'

A short conversation of that nature would, in nine cases out of ten, completely change a boy's attitude towards playing rugby. The application of psychology was very important in persuading boys to take part.

'The first boy to pass the finishing line in the 100 yards will be the fastest under-fifteen boy in school. Second, third and fourth boys will be in the relay team. Fancy going home tonight, boys, to say to your parents "I am the fastest boy in school" or "I am in the school's relay team"?'

An insignificant exercise of this nature, particularly with boys who felt they were beyond all hope, could change a boy's whole lifestyle. The fact that, for the first time in his life, he emerged a winner, however modest the opposition, very often awakened in him an ambition to participate more seriously in school games. His name would be mentioned in the school assembly, probably his first 'claim to fame'. This knowledge would be put to good use in the rugby season.

'Who were our sprinters in the summer, boys?'

The names would be given.

'Oh, yes, of course. They can play in the centre, or on the wing. We want speed there, lads, don't we?'

What made people such as myself want boys to play rugby? Rugby was not in *my* bones. The main influence was, of course, the environment. The type of lad I wanted as a companion *played the game*. Most importantly, it was the game played by the collier's son *and* the manager's son. High and low played it – those who lived in private houses and those who lived in council houses. The scholar and the non-academic. It was a game that opened doors which would otherwise remain shut. Rugby would help one to get on – and that was very important to the miner. To get on meant to get out; to get out of the influence of the colliery.

Most boys want to be good in one way or another. They want to be acclaimed. It is a boost for the morale. Do not all rugby players treasure their press cuttings? Fame at local, national or international level can be stimulating enough to drive one on to the next game.

Rugby is a game for making friends. Rugby is an institution, a means for playing and for socialising. It is a reason for travelling and visiting other rugby clubs, home and abroad. It is a means whereby one can meet the influential and the famous. It is a game worth playing. Rugby is an education.

Not only does rugby offer incentives of the kind mentioned above, some schoolmasters also teach fair play and sportsmanship, ingredients essential in a good man. They deliberately set out to teach boys the ethics of playing:

(a) to win with modesty and to lose graciously
(b) not to dispute the referee – 'He is right even though he could be wrong'
(c) to be sympathetic to an opponent when he has been injured
(d) not to be selfish
(e) playing the game in the true spirit
(f) giving the opponent the benefit of the doubt
(g) to be mentally and physically fit
(h) not to be fearful or cowardly
(i) to acquire skills, so as to give credit to oneself and the game
(j) to seek maximum enjoyment from every game
(k) to shake hands with one's opposite number after a game and say, 'Well done!'
(l) to seek to improve on every game played.

The contribution of schoolmasters towards the development of rugby in Wales at that time was immeasurable. Their loyalty, devotion and enthusiasm for the game were unequalled. They gave years of unstinted service in their leisure time to the furtherance of the game, in the hope that Wales would emerge as a winning rugby nation. In my own area men like John Morgan, McLeod Jones, Wyn Joseph, Ken Evans, Gwynfor and Hugh Davies, Jeff Reed, Bill Erith Jones, Gareth Thomas, Jeff Hopkin and many others, unheralded outside the Swansea Valley, gave decades of service with unflinching dedication.

Every valley in Wales had its own enthusiastic teachers whose ambition was for the improvement of senior rugby, so lamentably weak at the time. This collective and irresistible force in our schools paved the way for the euphoric '70s. The Swansea Valley committee at one stage had fourteen prospective headmasters in its ranks. It was an unwritten law that service on a schoolboy rugby committee was a high priority for every school-teacher who had ambitions to become a headmaster. There was a willingness to learn from each other. There was an oral tradition, handed down over the years. The 'tips', as they were called, are not available in coaching manuals.

I was very fortunate, for John Morgan of the Pontardawe Grammar School shared his meagre rugby facilities with me. From the day I arrived from college, John took an interest in me and was just the man to jostle me into teaching physical education correctly. There is no subject in the curriculum in which it is so easy to be indolent as PE; John and I can at least have the satisfaction of knowing that we did not succumb to that unprofessional attitude. Many a time we would remain long after school had finished, discussing any aspect which would be relevant to our work. Both of us firmly believed that the games lesson was not a 'go as you please' lesson, as it is in many schools today, but a lesson in which to teach boys how to play rugby properly.

Rugby masters in Wales are backroom boys. They are the workhorses. Their names rarely appear in newspaper print. In my time, some masters worked for five to eight years with boys, trying to instil in them a love of the game. They are, by nature, blinkered, oblivious to all but their profession. They are a soft touch, too! They work regularly at lunch-times. They stay after school to practise and play inter-school matches. They devote their Saturday mornings to school matches and their Saturday afternoons to schoolboy international trials. They attend schoolboy rugby meetings. They organise and travel to seven-a-side tournaments in England and Wales. They organise games. They referee, or arrange for a referee to appear; they arrange meals and buses. They organise raffles, discos and jumble sales, they buy and sell refreshments during school breaks, and they arrange sponsored walks in order to pay the rugby expenses. They supply and administer first aid. They take injured boys to their homes or to the hospital. They hold meetings with the boys. They provide jerseys, host visiting teams, do all this, and more – for what? One thing is certain – there is no extra money for the rugby master, not even out-of-pocket expenses. The WRU will grudgingly provide a dozen badly placed tickets for the home internationals, to be shared and sold to the rugby staff and school teams, which can be in excess of a dozen XVs. Scant reward for working regularly at the grass-roots of Welsh rugby. The teaching profession's contribution to rugby, unfortunately, has not been adequately recognised.

The teacher's love of the game is far more important than haggling for WRU status, and how long the WRU can continue to treat its most important servant in such a dismissive manner is a debatable point. I recall several long trips taken at home and abroad when, as teachers, we would rely heavily on the children's integrity and co-operation for a successful trip. They rarely let us down. In 1972 we ventured to take forty boys to Dortmund to play against the 19th and 22nd Regiments of the Royal Artillery. The exceptional Cwmtawe side remained unbeaten during the tour, boys playing against men in a type of game foreign to clubs in Wales.

When that tour came to an end, so did my days as a PE man. The new headmaster, Dr John Griffiths, offered me a promotion to year master. It was a situation I found it difficult to come to terms with, for I had devoted my whole teaching career to the furtherance of physical education, but it was a case of either take promotion with extra cash, or stay in a tracksuit until I was sixty-five. Family considerations prompted me to opt for the former. But Cwmtawe had an energetic PE staff in Geoff Davies, Gwyn Lewis and Gethin Edwards, whose combined zeal and devotion would ensure that Cwmtawe remained a formidable force in schoolboy sport. I soon realised that, as one began to distance oneself from active teaching, the increase in salary was never as satisfying a reward as the face of a boy in the process of learning or accomplishing something new.

When it became known that I had moved out of PE, a county councillor submitted my name for inclusion on the Welsh Sports Council. Much to his disappointment, he discovered that only councillors and members of certain associations were allowed to sit on the council. Knowledge and experience in sport were considered unnecessary factors.

There are diehards who still maintain that teachers, aptly named Corinthians, who specialise in subjects other than PE in the public, independent and some state schools were superior to the three-year-trained PE teachers in the state schools. Both, of course, contributed in their different ways. But there is one thing which should be obvious – a man who has been trained for three years, not only in the teaching of rugby but in fitness preparation as well, should be regarded as a better qualified person. Men who are graduates in French, maths and so forth are, to the world at large, experts in the subject of their degree. I have yet to meet a Corinthian with the rugby expertise to be bold enough to claim that they were better teachers of rugby than the qualified master – and I have taught with dozens of them in my time!

In my earlier days I used to take my subject to ridiculous extremes. 'Remember now, boys, your health is the best investment you can make. Take halibut oil capsules regularly in the winter to keep away sniffs and colds and not to miss rugby.' They used to follow my advice without question until the inevitable day when I returned to school after spending a few days at home with the flu, to be greeted by one of the wags in the classroom. 'Are you better, sir? Did you forget to take your halibut oil capsules?' he asked, to the delight of his classmates.

I felt a concern for the pupils beyond the needs of duty, especially in the case of a potential star on whom I used to impress the value of sleeping regular hours, eating steak, good food and milk and abstaining from drinking beer.

I remember Carwyn James playing his first game for Llanelli at Pontypool while still a schoolboy. I was on the wing that day. That game proved to be a tough baptism for him into the ranks of first-class rugby. He had every reason to be nervous, for he was playing against one of the most committed wing forwards of the day in Alan Forward (Pontypool and Wales). He did not have an easy passage, but showed some definite touches which augured well for the future. On the way home that evening, the captain of the Llanelli team, Ossie Williams, stopped the bus in Aberdare and invited the players and committee to join him for a beer. Carwyn, who was sitting with me in the back row, did not budge.

'Come on, Carwyn and Bill,' shouted Ossie.

'No, thank you, Ossie,' said Carwyn. 'I'm staying here.'

'What about you, Bill?'

'No thanks, Os.'

I was sympathetic to Carwyn's refusal because of his youth. I decided to keep him company. However, a few minutes later, after the bus had cleared, Carwyn stood up and said, 'Let's go and have a drink somewhere else, but not with the members of the team.'

'I thought you didn't drink?' I questioned.

'I do. But it's very important not to do so in front of certain committee members because of their strong religious beliefs; they object to young players drinking beer.' It would be ridiculous to suggest such restraint nowadays, for drink has become an acceptable part of the rugby scene.

Carwyn's astute observation was given to me in the form of a tip which I thought worth passing on to youngsters on the verge of achieving a name for themselves in sport. Little did I know, at the time, that Carwyn would become one of the most revered rugby commentators in the world, a man whose eloquence and profound knowledge of the game reserved for him a golden chapter in its history. His greatest attribute was his humility. He understood that it was impossible to have an expert knowledge in every facet of the game. He realised that physical development and fitness were specialist areas, and that the intricacies of forward play were sometimes foreign to him. His ideology was a simple one: given the right players, blessed with basic skills, in a free-running game, winning rugby was always possible, as was evidenced in the 1971 British Lions tour. His rugby was an artistic, disciplined adventure, where the rogue and the thug had no part.

How things have changed! At one time one could more or less guarantee a boy would remain uninjured if he followed his lessons properly. The plague of injuries that has occurred in rugby recently is a distressing business. It is not a very pleasant experience to take a boy to hospital and to his home after a dislocation or a fracture. It's amazing to what lengths dirty players will go to maim opponents, and in my opinion scrum-half is the most vulnerable position. I have seen a scrum-half deliberately kick the hand of an opponent instead of the ball when he is about to pass the ball off the ground, and the same player hacking, with the side of his hand, the wrists of his opponent to reduce the efficiency of his passing. Can you imagine the mentality of a player digging his heel into an unsuspecting hand while it is on the ground? And the list does not end there. Why should an innocent player not be warned of heinous characters who hide behind a façade of sportsmanship? There are too many players nowadays who are intent on wrecking the ethos of a great game.

I have always found the 'big boys' a fascinating study. John Charles, the great Welsh soccer star, was known as the 'Gentle Giant'. Rhys Williams, Alan Martin and Delme Thomas, the former Wales and Lions lock forwards, are genuinely amiable fellows who must have had to adopt an aggression contrary to their nature in order to play rugby.

143

Because Jim, one of the boys at school, was an orphan and had been blessed with foster-parents who doted on him, I felt an obligation to pay him more attention than was usual. He too was a good-natured, large fellow and, try as I would, I could never get him even to pretend to be nasty. To cap it all, he had been selected to appear in an Under-Fifteen final trial for Wales. I had completely failed to infuse aggression into his play, but the solution of the problem came to me one night. I decided to seek the advice of an expert, a former British Lion whom I knew quite well. Much to my relief, he agreed to meet me. I met him in a pub in Swansea. After a while we came to the purpose of the meeting.

'Let me, first of all, tell you what I know about the second-row position and afterwards you can fill in the important parts which I have missed out,' I said.

He nodded his head in agreement.

Some fifteen minutes later, after I had exhausted my knowledge, I asked him if he would give me the benefit of his experience. He looked at me and said, quite frankly, 'I didn't know there was so much to the position, myself.'

It was then I realised that many international players play their game naturally, with no expert knowledge, just an instinct for the game and plenty of experience. They could certainly play to world level, but their own perception of the game might be very limited indeed. However, the night was not a complete failure, because my friend did reveal in conversation some ways of developing aggression – ways which cannot be printed!

When I told Jim that the great former Lion was watching his rugby career with interest, he bucked up his ideas and worked a lot harder. There is a Welsh proverb which typifies Jim's character perfectly – 'A lamb will never be a bear'. He never got into the Welsh team, but people remind me now and again what a nice chap he was, and that is better than an international cap dishonourably worn.

It is important also to remind good players to be careful of their relationships with other people.

'Things have changed for you. People will want to know you because you are different. It is imperative, therefore, that you have your feet firmly on the ground. Your behaviour must be an example to the other boys.'

If they had been awarded international caps I felt it was my duty to show them how to prepare speeches and to coach them to deliver with style. Small Welsh-speaking villages want to recognise their young heroes. The local rugby club, the chapel or church society, or the welfare committee have been known to be generous in their acknowledgement of the star products of the area. Therefore, it is an obligation on the boy's part to try to respond with dignity with a word of thanks to those who were kind enough to present him with either a suitably inscribed painting or a studio-taken photograph of himself; a token which will remind him for the rest of his days of the kindness of his community when they deemed him worthy of their esteem for bringing honour to the village.

These were some of the concerns which occupied my time and thoughts during the days of PE teaching. The post-war teachers with a vision of a new philosophy in physical education saw the result of their ideals come to fruition in the '60s. Then, hundreds of masters who had expended their time, knowledge and energy establishing that foundation, suddenly found that the success of the educational sports system was not credited to them, but to the WRU coaching system. Every Welsh victory was a victory for coaches, and the schoolmasters' contribution towards that era was never acknowledged or appreciated. Coaching became the panacea for Welsh rugby problems. It did not matter that Alan Martin, Barry John, Gerald and Mervyn Davies, Maurice Richards and so forth had grown and developed within a 'natural' system; the glory was claimed by the WRU. Coaches became superior to the brigade of professionally trained men.

What would have happened, I wonder, if all teachers of rugby had joined WRU clubs as coaches? There were clubs anxious to entice schoolmasters to coach long before the coaching system was introduced. For my own part, in addition to being asked to coach in the south of France in 1952, I was asked by Llanelli in 1957 and Aberavon at a later date, and by other clubs many times since. But my chosen vocation, like that of many others, was teaching, which I enjoyed. It is impossible to serve two masters. My allegiance was to the school. To give this up for coaching a first-class club twice a week and watching them play, in addition to forgoing inter-school games, was too much of a sacrifice for me.

Chapter Eleven

Giant-Killer

In the late '60s, political implications began to stir the tranquil and successful rhythm of the tripartite system of the six secondary schools of the Swansea Valley. At the wave of a wand the six schools became one, creating what must have been the longest school in the world, over ten miles long with school buildings in Gwaun-cae-gurwen, Pontardawe and Clydach. Swansea Valley children became the victims of a political ideology. I was of the opinion that comprehensive education, properly administered, was the perfect answer to the needs of secondary education, but that bout of enthusiasm was soon dispelled when I realised that the transition to a twelve-form-entry school meant, in effect, a greater concentration on academic subjects. It did not take long for the children to realise that the top five classes were 'bright' (in the academic sense), and that the seven other classes were in some way 'inferior'. The spirit of the 11+, under a new guise, remained firmly in place.

The children still suffer from that decision of the authorities. They have to trudge, not from one classroom to another, but from one classroom in a school to a classroom in one of three other schools (for that is what they were seventeen years ago). Given the volume of rain which falls in the Swansea Valley, many of them are drenched to the skin throughout the day. The school has been visited by LEA officers, HMIs and councillors, who seem to be completely oblivious to its distressful nature.

The vocational type of education provided by the technical school was considered to be undignified and unappealing, with the result that it was discontinued, or downgraded. The technical subjects were removed from the curriculum. It did not matter that former Tech students were making an indispensable contribution to the needs of industry. It was deemed wrong for working-class children to learn work skills and thought that a dose of memory training, as provided for the bright children, would open up new possibilities for them. Some time ago I received a letter from an old boy of the Tech whose name was John Duncan Davies, OBE, MSc, PhD, DSc, CEng, FICE, MIStrucE. He had worked as an engineer, building bridges, superstructures, motorways and so on, before embarking on a career in teaching at university level. He eventually became the Principal of Glamorgan University.

In 1997 Gareth was nominated as the world's best ever rugby player, even better than the great David Campese and Zin Zan Brooke of Australia and New Zealand respectively, which was praise indeed. John Duncan, Gareth and many others are splendid examples of the success that can be achieved after being given a second chance.

There is, however, no mention of restoring the Tech to Pontardawe. Having set the example long ago, its people continue to be deprived of the education that is part and parcel of the Valley's heritage. Years after the establishment of the Tech, the Tory government was ecstatic when it announced its pioneering establishment of new city technology colleges. What was considered good for children then had been considered bad for the Swansea Valley in 1969 when their technical school had been taken away from them by the Labour Party's comprehensive ideology.

The combination of all the secondary schools into one instantly made it a school worthy of meeting any school in Great Britain on equal terms in the game of rugby. The catchment area was a hive of rugby activity, with village teams such as Vardre, Pontardawe, Glais, Trebanos, Alltwen, Ystalyfera, Cwmllynfell, Cwmtwrch, Brynamman and Cwmgors, each with a story to tell. In the past the large grammar schools had dominated schoolboy rugby in Wales. With the advent of the comprehensive school, that reign was soon to be challenged. What is curious about that period of domination was the fact that it was the small school that nurtured the players with flair.

Tanner and Davies, Onllwyn Brace and Lewis Jones (Gowerton), Carwyn James, Ken Jones, Barry John, Gareth Davies and Jonathan Davies (Gwendraeth), Cliff Morgan (Tonyrefail) and Claude Davey

(Ystalyfera) are examples of players who were bred in small schools. The reason for this might be that the better player of the small school would have to develop flair, particularly in a weak team, to learn to cover the less able during a game against a team comprising bigger players. Boys of a bigger stature did not necessarily have to develop survival skills, because their size would bulldoze them through their smaller rivals.

It was not long before Cwmtawe, according to *Rothman's Rugby Union Yearbook*, was recognised as a team full of talent and one that had established itself as one of the leading 'nurseries' in the game. *The Rugby World* named it as one of the three leading rugby schools in Great Britain. Even though I have been involved with boys from this area for over thirty years, I was not surprised to discover that a small village like Trebanos could produce sportsmen of the calibre of Bleddyn Bowen (Wales and South Wales Police), Robert Jones (British Lions, Wales and Swansea), Arwel Thomas (Wales and Swansea) and cricket player Greg Thomas (England and Glamorgan), a fast bowler. They are custodians of a tradition, and as such possess qualities which are inborn rather than acquired, particularly in their fearless competitiveness and relentless perseverance.

When Cwmtawe became a comprehensive, a county councillor said to me, 'I expect that, as head of PE, you have soccer teams in the school?'

'Better an empty purse than an empty head,' I said to myself. He did not comprehend that PE teachers had an insatiable drive to see children play; the sport itself did not matter. However, the writing was on the wall and rugby lost its monopoly as boys began to pick and choose from a selection of physical activities as diverse as fishing and golf. It did not matter as far as Cwmtawe was concerned, for rugby remained a force there. It was not the case in many schools, however, where rugby lost its dominant role in favour of other options. One master complained to me that he bussed his complete sixth form to a sports centre to engage in a plethora of physical activities. Only a few wanted to play rugby. Many schools were in difficulties. 'We'll fulfil the fixture providing we can include members of our local youth team,' said a disillusioned master of a large comprehensive school to me. With the open option system of physical education, some schools could not play against their traditional rivals; they were simply not strong enough. In the season 1953–54 the schools used to play between fifteen and twenty fixtures a season. By 1986, many schools were overdoing it when they extended their fixture lists to thirty-five matches and beyond. Schoolboy rugby was caught up in the exuberance of the trend, following the example of first-class clubs by playing too much rugby.

Happily, in the early '70s schools were not under such duress, particularly when two of the finest rugby schools in the United Kingdom, Neath and Cwmtawe, were in opposition. These games used to produce large crowds in schoolboy terms, for both sides contained future household names in rugby.

I remember phoning Jeff Kelleher, the international referee from St Athan, to invite him to referee one of our home matches against Neath.

'I am sorry,' he said. 'I don't referee schoolboy matches.' His point-blank refusal deflated me.

'You have never refereed a schoolboy match, Mr Kelleher?' I asked.

'That's right,' he answered.

'You honestly surprise me. What if the WRU heard of your incomplete refereeing experience?' I said, quietly pulling his leg.

'All right then,' he replied. 'Since I am refereeing in Milford Haven in the afternoon, I might as well try my luck in the morning with the schoolboys.'

'That is all we need, a neutral referee, and you are unknown to both the Neath rugby master and myself.'

After the match, I went to his room to pay his expenses.

'No, thanks. Put the money in the sports fund or something. I should be paying you for inviting me to referee the game this morning. It was unbelievable. I never realised such talent existed. I have never experienced such a game. It was probably the best game I've ever refereed, better than any first-class or any international match.'

'You need to come more often, Mr Kelleher,' I replied.

'No, seriously, not one of my decisions was queried and there was not a nasty incident in the match. To cap it all, both captains shook my hand and thanked me for refereeing. Any time you want me, just give me a ring.'

Before the educational reorganisation, hardly any Under-Fourteen rugby was played in our schools. It was entirely different at Under-Fifteen level, for there was an unyielding enthusiasm from dedicated masters for inter-school and districts rugby, ranging from Newport, Pembrokeshire, to Newport, Monmouth.

'I do not remember playing rugby until I was fifteen,' said Rhys Williams (British Lions and Wales). 'But once I started there was no holding me back.'

I remember submitting two articles to the *Western Mail* in 1976, expressing fears about the exclusive concentration on rugby for boys in many of our junior schools. Time and time again I have seen examples which prove conclusively that rugby is a 'big boy's' game up to the age of sixteen. Boys who mature at the age of eleven, with the physical characteristics of boys of fifteen, can dominate any rugby game at a young age because of their maturity, only to experience the painful realisation that, at sixteen, the victims of the past have grown to outmatch them in size and skill.

As I see it, early specialisation in rugby could be the death-knell of the game. The function of a junior school is to provide a basic physical education programme including swimming, gymnastics and basic skills for all games. The headmaster, PE adviser and HMI should never allow one game to monopolise the PE period. Their duty, as educationists, is to protect the children from those well-meaning, often misguided teachers anxious to further the cause of one game. If a master wants to teach one game exclusively, he should do so after school, with the parents' permission. If parents are keen, they should encourage their local rugby club to provide the facility.

I have always found, with a few exceptions, that boys who play rugby are models of good behaviour. With boys who have started young, however, much to my dismay, I have found too many branded by their teachers as bullies because of their early training in rugby aggression. There is an attempt, in some cases, to make men out of boys. I asked an eleven-year-old boy who had appeared in his first ever game in a schools' district trial what position he was playing.

'Centre,' he said, quite proudly.

'Oh, very good,' I said. 'What is your job?'

'When we are in an attacking position I am supposed to take the ball on the run, and pass it on the inside to the full-back, who is coming into the line on the burst.'

I looked at him in amazement. 'You are pulling my leg,' I said.

'No I am not, sir,' he said.

To assimilate a difficult ploy of that nature would take years of practice, but his young teacher's motto seemed to be 'Never mind the basic skills; let's get on with the game'. A little knowledge of rugby can be very dangerous.

Another unnecessary feature of the game is the 'psyching up' of boys before a match. It is a clarion-call more fitting to a war than to a game. 'Keep your wind for the game, boy!' would be an apt retort from members of the old school of teaching.

As parents and teachers we need to keep our children children as long as we can. To provide them with adult ideas and practices and venture to hasten their maturity for the glorification of rugby is foolish. The game can be sold to boys when they are ready for it, and not before. One cannot afford to lose *one* potential player at an early age. Parents can be very demanding at this level, especially if their offspring happens to be remarkably talented. As one would expect, however, not all parents are enamoured of the game.

'I don't want my son to play rugby,' said a mother to me, very forcefully.

'Rugby is great fun,' I said. 'I would not have missed it for the world.'

She broke in, 'In your day there was no need to pay insurance. Why should he play? To get cauliflower ears? To fracture bones and pull muscles? To become a paraplegic and blame me for the rest of his days for not stopping him? The game has got out of hand; the fun has gone out of it. Watch TV on Sunday. The game has become too commercial. The Union has lost its feeling for the players. The player is no longer supreme; he's become a sacrifice for the shekels of petrol, insurance and paint. His importance on the field has been replaced by the captions of the sponsoring companies.'

Rugby has become a casualty of the affluent society. Children on average watch four hours of television a day. Many children have been guided into pursuits which do not involve physical contact – golf, tennis, sailing, horse-riding, etc. Another factor worth taking into account is the gradual change that has taken place in rugby-playing villages. The care of the young was at one time the responsibility of the community. Nowadays there is a natural fear of allowing children to be unsupervised in the old play areas. One can walk the length and breadth of our village these days and not see a child at play anywhere. In the '50s and '60s there were patches of ground where children used to play regularly in Cwmgors and Gwaun-cae-gurwen. These days there are no children playing in groups. What was once a regular feature of village life has disappeared. There has been a catastrophic change in social behaviour. It is incredible that nowadays the majority of boys do not want to play cricket, soccer and rugby in their leisure time. They do not need to rely on games for entertainment, for they live in the age of advanced technology where videos, music centres and computers are available to all social classes.

Once the small communities of Wales lose their seemingly irrepressible appetite for rugby football, one can confidently assert that the game of rugby will die in Wales.

I was warden of the youth centre at Gwaun-cae-gurwen in the late '50s and '60s, when rugby was at its pinnacle of popularity in Wales. With me at the centre as assistant warden was Ieuan Evans, former coach of Welsh Youth, Llanelli and Swansea. Ieuan's passion was rugby football, especially youth rugby. He revelled in it. Young men from a wide area came to practise there; such was the demand on occasion that he would take thirty players on one pitch whilst I took thirty on the other pitch. At the end of sixteen happy years both of us decided to call it a day because the educational system did not stimulate enough interest in games. The captain of the youth team expressed the changing attitudes perfectly: 'I play rugby to get fit. I don't agree with you that I should get fit to play rugby.'

Ieuan and I had a big laugh about it, but we realised that change was inevitable and that the young player's assertion was contrary to the ethos of two diehards such as ourselves. There is no doubt at all that the small communities of Wales have been the backbone of Welsh rugby. It is there that the vast majority of the great stars have been weaned and nurtured, not in the towns and cities. When I went to live in Cwmgors in 1955 it seemed that everyone belonged to the rugby club in one way or another, as players, ex-players, committee men, ticket-seller, linesman, trainer, coach, secretary, bus-driver, reporter, jersey-washer, president, patron, vice-president – all proud to belong. It was the time when international tickets were at a premium.

Rugby included all sorts. Men who supposedly knew nothing about history would suddenly achieve eminence for their knowledge about the history of the game.

'Name a Welsh rugby XV all beginning with W,' I was asked on one occasion.

'Gerwyn Williams, Les Williams, Bleddyn Williams,' I replied, then faltered.

'Fancy not knowing our Welsh rugby history, boys, and him being a PE teacher too.'

I cringed whenever I saw the man who had asked me the question. He was a typical Welsh supporter, an expert on one facet of the game, and for that he held a revered place in the fellowship of rugby.

In some instances, too, loyalty to the club could be taken to ridiculous extremes. The son of the local rugby reporter, a modest full-back for the village XV, always had a write-up. Without fail, he was 'outstanding' one week, 'brilliant' the next, along with 'excellent', 'a great custodian', 'on his own', 'tremendous', 'magnificent'. The father would describe his son's play in that way for seven weeks and then start again, using the same descriptive words for the next seven, and so it continued until his son decided to move to another club out of sheer embarrassment.

The reporter's life centred on the club. It was his passion. Whenever anyone died in the village, he would find a rugby connection. 'Tom, the brother of Wil and Dai Thomas, was buried last week. Tom nearly played rugby for the Second XV as a reserve; not like his brothers, who were stars of the First XV.'

'Mrs Annie Davies, the neighbour of Mrs Beatrice Jones, the rugby club's jersey-washer, passed away last Thursday. She will be missed by the club for she used to share the ironing of the jerseys with Mrs Jones.'

Change is inevitable, of course. Now many young people join the rugby social club to play bingo, one-armed bandits, darts, snooker, pool and so on.

'I sip my pint and play my game,' said a corpulent young member of a rugby club to me, slapping his wide girth with his hands.

'Why, do you mean to tell me that a big lad like you does not play?'

'It's a mug's game. I'd rather stay indoors in the warm.'

'The game has become too demanding, with too many training sessions and too many games,' some players complain.

On the other hand, there are players who are prepared to adopt a professional attitude towards training and playing. A substantial number will train throughout the year, play over sixty games a season, and enjoy every minute of it. 'I don't watch rugby any more. All teams, whatever the level, play the same. You can pick twenty-five different wing forwards to play for Wales. Not one will be better than any other.'

The individuality has gone out of the game. There is too much stress and too early an emphasis on competition, especially for cups and shields. The result has become more important than the game. At one time physical education was a very popular subject to teach, but over the years it has lost its glamour because of the pitiful wages teachers have been given. How can a teacher aged thirty-three be happy when he is not even earning the average national wage?

Was it any wonder, therefore, that a great number of ex-internationals and first-class players left the profession for television, insurance, business, banking, etc.? Not only have the schools lost their famous PE teachers, they have also lost many of them within the framework of the school by promotion to administrative posts.

There is no magic formula for rugby success; it comes only from people who understand the complexities of the game and from positive planning. Original thinkers are needed and they are very, very rare. Lamenting recent results and glorifying the past won't change the present or the future. But it *is* possible to have another golden era, not by wishful thinking, but by adopting a national policy which will ensure that the first decade in the new millennium will outshine the achievements of the '70s.

There has been a vociferous demand within the WRU to dismiss schoolboy rugby and replace it with club rugby. Some clubs cannot, at the moment, field second teams or youth teams. How could they manage to organise the age groups which are now under the jurisdiction of the school?

The new measures adopted for physical education by the government in its 1985 publication *Better Schools* do not include a national policy for the teaching of PE. Instead, Local Education Authorities are allowed the freedom to exercise their own policies. This is a clear mistake, for health, exercise and high physical performance are *essential* in raising our standards in competition at international level, as well as being an investment in our nation's health and well-being. Should we not be alarmed when our children become obese, lethargic and badly postured, and shy away from physical exercise? From my experience, accountability is essential in order to create excellence in physical education. In my opinion, the government must adopt and implement a national policy in order to establish this.

In the early '70s Mr Onllwyn Brace, from BBC TV, asked Goronwy Morgan, of Llandovery College, and me to express our views regarding the state of the game in Wales. I suppose we could have joined in the fervour of acclamation at the time. Instead, we relayed some of the danger signals we had experienced and emphasised the need to plan ahead so as to retain our ascendency. Who wanted to listen to such prophets of doom? It was the zenith of Wales's achievement. Wales was winning. Coaches became more revered than Welsh preachers, singers and actors. A coaching certificate became a treasure. Students of PE, young teachers, ex-players, snapped up the magic qualification which would enable them to produce winning teams playing champagne rugby every Saturday afternoon. There was a fear that coaches would outnumber players. Alas, rugby is not an easy game. How can one cope in a gymnasium without a PE qualification? I remember asking a teacher in Cwmtawe if he would consider helping me with rugby. Without batting an eyelid he said, 'No thanks.' Not to be outdone, I said, 'You are a funny one. I remember you playing for the school. A few teachers gave up their time for you.'

'That's not the point,' he replied. 'I was a prop, who bent my back to go into the scrum, kept my head up and my legs apart, and shoved. I stood in the lineouts, supporting or blocking the jumper, or chasing if we lost the ball. That was my contribution to the game in school, university and my club. I knew nothing else about the game and now you want me to take charge of a school team. Not likely – they know more about it than I do. It would be a case of the blind leading the blind.'

I was taken aback by this truthful answer, but I had no alternative but to accept his point of view.

Chapter Twelve

Rewards

Teachers do not expect rewards, because it is their duty to educate the children in their charge, but it's gratifying when some of them offer, in various ways, a token of their regard. The most unusual token for me came about in this way. Many years ago I wanted to rewire the electrical supply of my house. I wanted it done quickly, because of the danger involved. I made enquiries, and discovered that an old pupil, whom I had not seen for years, was prepared to do it at a price which had not been disclosed. He came cheerfully, armed with the tools of his trade. He worked busily every evening until late at night for a week until the job was finished. 'The end of the song is the penny,' says a popular Welsh proverb.

'How much do I owe you?' I asked.

'Do you remember the Urdd gymnastic club you used to hold every Monday evening from three forty-five to five thirty?'

'Yes, indeed. Quite popular it was too.'

'I agree wholeheartedly. I spent three years in that gym club with you, and enjoyed every minute of it.'

'Thank you. That's nice to recall.'

'You did not receive any payment for Urdd work, did you?'

'Not a penny. Only the love of the sport and for the Urdd, you know. I enjoyed it.'

'That's what I thought,' he said. 'But it's my turn now. Here is the bill for the materials, which you'll have to pay, but as for the labour charges, you can forget them.'

'Hey, come off it, don't be stupid. Name your price like everybody else.'

'If you should want me in future, I shall expect you to pay.'

'Oh come on now,' I repeated. 'Don't be outrageous.'

'No, no,' he said adamantly, 'I have been waiting for a chance to repay you for those great nights in the gym.'

That was a touching gesture if ever there was one. But the story doesn't end there. When Cwmtawe School became a comprehensive, rugby referees were in short supply. By sheer accident I met the electrician with the Samaritan spirit and suggested to him that he should take up refereeing.

'I've never thought of myself as a referee,' he said.

'Start off with the Seconds next Saturday and as long as you're honest, you'll become a regular referee. But if I find you showing favour to Cwmtawe, you won't be asked again.'

'But I don't know the rules,' he said anxiously.

'That's no problem,' I said, and handed him a schoolboy book of rugby rules.

'Know those backwards, and you won't go wrong. Knowledge of the rules and honesty are the ingredients necessary to make a top-class referee.'

He was the first on the rugby field that Saturday morning. He was re-reading the rules when I arrived.

'I must say you are very keen,' I said cheerfully. 'Aren't you familiar with the saying that a referee is right, even though he's wrong?'

'I am determined to be fair to both sides,' he said with conviction. And indeed, when Winston Jones did become an international referee, no one could accuse him of being dishonest. He was certainly different from one famous referee who, prior to a school game, asked, 'Which way do you want the game to go, Bill?' *He* was not asked again.

And pupils' dependence on teachers extended beyond school life too. I recall now how Gareth Edwards expected me to write all his speeches for him. Glan, his father, used to call and ask if Gareth's speech was ready, whether Gareth was in Scotland, Ireland or Canada. It was difficult to write about a match that had not been played, especially a winning and losing speech! But wherever he spoke, he was always sure of an apt quotation – in Welsh, of course – even against New Zealand and Canada.

'Remember, Gareth, that God has given us the gift of a language. Always try to gain respect and support for it. We are only a few, mind, but we are something special.'

He was asked many years ago to be a guest speaker somewhere in Gwent, and in a panic he telephoned me one morning. 'I'm in desperate trouble; I'm supposed to speak on the theme that rugby is the religion of the Welsh, whilst the local cleric is to speak on Christianity as being the religion of the Welsh. I'm supposed to be funny. Can you help me?' he implored anxiously.

'For how long do you want to speak?' I asked.

'About twenty minutes to half an hour?' he asked, hopefully.

'Good gracious me!' I said. 'I could manage ten minutes, but half an hour – well!'

'Oh, Bill, I am depending on you. I need it by tomorrow.'

There it was, a typical Edwards request. I was saddled with his problem. During the course of the morning, I shared a free period in the staff room with a colleague, the Reverend Dr Elwyn Davies, who noticed that I was absorbed in my thoughts.

'Something troubling you, Bill?' he asked.

I informed him of my dilemma. He sportingly assured me that he would think about the proposal during his lunch-hour. Dr Elwyn, who was already writing songs and scripts for famous Welsh artists, including the only song Gareth himself ever recorded, returned after lunch on that critical day and produced a sheet of greaseproof paper on which were written some indecipherable words which he started reading to me, to see whether they were worthy to be included in the speech.

'Gentlemen, I propose to prove that the first religion of the Welsh is rugby, and these words, mark you, are not mine, they were the words of a minister to his congregation on a certain Sunday morning. He himself had been to an international match the previous Saturday, and had been really impressed. There were about seven in that congregation on that particular Sunday, when he got up into the pulpit and said, "My friends, I went to see a game yesterday. You ask what game? There *is* only one game, dear friends, and that is rugby football. I went there because I had heard so much about winning points, Triple Crowns and conversions. I went to see what they were all about, and what I saw brought me to the conclusion that this big congregation was better than mine.

In what way, you ask? Well, I will tell you, dear friends. First, the place was full, even the gallery, long before it was due to start. Secondly, everyone had paid in advance for his seat. Thirdly, everyone was there on time. Fourthly, they sang hymns beautifully, even without hymnals, yes, indeed, without an organ, and to celebrate the occasion I even saw a group having communion in a corner. And you should have seen the fifteen disciples, ladies and gentlemen, with their coats off and running all over the place. But no, my people, they knew how to run together and how to share the ball as they passed to each other and knew how to keep to the rules of the game. If one transgressed, there would be a huge shrill of the whistle and all the eyes in the stadium would be focused on the transgressor.

Before I conclude my sermon this morning, I should like to read to you the ten commandments of rugby.

I am Rugger, thy sport, which brought thy country out of the land of darkness and disrepute, into the light of popularity. Thou shalt have no other sport beside me.

Thou shalt not make thyself a graven image of Rugger, even in the likeness of rounders or cricket, nor in the likeness of marbles, nor soccer, nor any other similar silly game within thy pitch or backyard.

Remember thy Saturday to keep it holy for me. Five days shalt thou work and do all thy fiddles. On Saturday, thy wife shall not drive thee into thy garden, nor scullery, nor to do her shopping, nor visit her mother, for this day is Rugger Day.

Honour all thy Rugger committees and coaches that thou mayest live long to have all the tickets thou needest.

Thou shalt not call the referee names, save when he is not fair to thy side.

Thou shalt not create a nuisance with rattles and toilet papers unless thou hast the larger ones.

Thou shalt not sing dirty songs unless thou knowest the same properly.

Thou shalt not bear false witness against thy side, nor thy committee, unless it be colourful and convincing.

Thou shalt not harbour any thoughts in thy head save Rugger.

Thou shalt think of Rugger even when thou art in bed with thy wife, when thou art eating chips or sitting on thy toilet, or when thou listenest to thy wife's preaching on Saturday night or to the preacher on Sunday morning. Thou shalt think of me and me only, because I am a jealous game and need thee all for myself.'"

Gareth had his speech, and a bit more. How he fared, I don't know even to this day.

I would maintain now that one of his biggest contributions was to the Swansea Valley. I suggested to him once that it would be a good exercise in public relations if he and Barry John played for the school in a charity match against a Cwmtawe Old Boys side, which itself figured star players. That first match brought a crowd of over five thousand. The game was to kick off at six, and Barry John had not yet been seen. I was in a state of panic. At six fifteen he arrived, breathless.

'I've been in the village for more than an hour. The traffic was so congested, I could not get through,' he said.

Pontardawe had never seen such a crowd. The following day a local publican rang me to say that he had sold more beer that night than he did normally in a month. No wonder he was keen to know when the next match was due! That match was the first of many.

Dave (Dai) Duckham and John Spencer of England and Lions fame came the following year, and what a popular draw-card they proved to be.

'It's years since I have played with the spectators standing on the touchline,' said Dave, with apparent pleasure.

'Any time you want us down, Bill, we'll come without expenses,' were John's last words to me.

Gerald Davies never missed one of those matches. Mervyn Davies, J.P.R., J.J. Williams, Phil Bennett, Dai Morris, Alan Martin and a host of native Swansea Valley first-class players made the occasion into a memorable annual event.

One evening, after one of the matches, Gareth was asked at the Glanafon Hotel, where he was guest speaker, which of the four Welsh outside-halfs he had played with was the best.

'I was too young, really, to assess the merits of David Watkins. Some say Barry John made me. I would like to think that I helped him a bit too! As for Phil Bennett, you saw how great he was in South Africa on the film we saw tonight. John Bevan, Aberavon RFC, has already played two exciting games in France and England. I consider myself very fortunate to have had the honour of playing with the four of them.'

Harry Hallesey, the head of English at Cwmtawe, wrote a tribute to him in one of the match programmes, saying, 'As natives of this area, we can be forgiven if we reflect that the one common factor in these famous partnerships was Gareth. You cannot make bricks without straw, or great outside-halfs without partners of the same class. When some eminent historian looks back on his record-breaking career, his verdict may be expressed in words that would never occur to this most modest of men. Off the field he was content to give praise to others; on the field he was the greatest of them all.'

I recall, with mixed emotions, another difficult situation in which I found myself, thanks to the fame of Gareth Edwards. The telephone rang one evening.

'Is that Mr Bill Samuel?' asked a pleasant female voice.

'It is,' I replied.

'Is there anyone nearby listening to this conversation?' she asked. This was strange, I thought to myself. I replied that there wasn't.

'I am Marilyn Gaunt from Thames Television. Could I arrange a meeting with you, Bill?' was her next question. Instantly I was on my guard.

'Are you sure there is no one listening in to our chat?' she repeated. By now I was alarmed at her insistence on secrecy. This time I was more deliberate and asked her the nature of the call. She hedged again, and with caution she divulged that she had to see me and that we would have to arrange a meeting-place before she could reveal the nature of her request. She assured me that everything was above board and asked me to meet her at seven thirty in the Castle Hotel, Neath, on the following Tuesday. By this time I felt sorry for the girl, because she had conveyed to me that she was sincere. So as not to prolong the agony, I agreed to her request.

'Looking forward to seeing you on Tuesday, then, Bill,' she said as a parting shot.

When I returned to the sitting-room and told Velda that I was off on a blind date on the following Tuesday, she was more incredulous than I. We both had a good laugh and looked forward with expectation to Tuesday night.

The Castle Hotel in Neath is a familiar meeting-place and so it was that evening when I waited patiently amongst a number of men who had come for a meeting of some society or other. But I was not looking for a man, but for a woman with an educated voice. How does one go about approaching a stranger one does not know except by her voice? I felt acutely awkward standing there, no drink in my hand, the occasional man looking at me rather curiously. But I was in my best suit and prepared for anything. When she finally arrived, armed with luggage, she walked right over to me and shook my hand warmly. She apologised for being late and asked me to excuse her while she booked in at reception and took her luggage upstairs. She would have a wash and brush-up and would meet me in the small bar where we could have a drink together.

When I was alone I realised that some of the men were giving me questioning looks. I could feel myself blushing in response to the sudden guilt which came over me. The mysterious voice had blossomed into a very striking and attractive young blonde and here was I – or so it seemed – lying in wait for her. I sensed an air of suspicion on one or two faces.

Fifteen minutes later she came bustling in, armed with an attaché case, and sat down alongside me. We talked for a while about her journey and then she came to the point. Before she did so, she looked around furtively and spoke in a whisper. She had been sent to do research for *This Is Your Life* on Gareth Edwards. They were hoping to feature him on the programme and my name had been given as one of the people who had made a major contribution to his career. Would I be interested in being considered as a possible recruit for the TV show?

I had, in the past, done many embarrassing things for the cause of Gareth Edwards and here was another – to be included on a programme which was watched by millions. The thought was terrifying, but for the sake of the Edwards family I agreed to be considered. In my reply I had raised my voice and my young, attractive companion suddenly asserted that the small bar was too public and that she was afraid that snippets of our conversation could be heard by the increasing number of people in the hotel. Would I go up to her bedroom?

I was horrified and began to make excuses. No one could possibly be listening. She was adamant, however, so sheepishly I agreed. The young lady led the way out of the small bar, along the hallway and up the stairs with yours truly in her wake. I wished the floor would open up and swallow me, such was my ordeal. Were there any men there that night from the Swansea Valley? I could hear the gossip: 'Bill Samuel, the schoolmaster, going upstairs to a bedroom with a pretty young blonde.'

It was a relief when we found the privacy of her bedroom and she started asking questions. She wrote furiously for more than an hour until I had exhausted my knowledge of Gareth Edwards. When it was all finished, she informed me that she would have to type the stories and then submit them to the producer who would, along with the stories given by others, select the more interesting ones for inclusion in the programme. The stories which had something special to say would be edited by their experts to convey the whole story of his life. She assured me that I had every chance of inclusion. Little did she know that I was by no means keen. In due course she would inform me either way, but if I was successful, a return ticket and a two-night booking at a five-star hotel in London would be forwarded. She implored me not to mention our meeting.

Some weeks went by, and in due course Gareth's father, his brother-in-law Clive and I were on that train with first-class tickets to take part in *This Is Your Life*. The secrecy surrounding the programme is unbelievable. We were not allowed outside our rooms. We went to the studios for a rehearsal, all except Gareth and Eamonn Andrews, of course. We were given scripts and, for the first time, we knew our stories and the sequence of appearance. On the day of the actual production we were confined to the limits of a private room where we found a generous supply of all we needed in the way of food and drink. My wife had included in my luggage a special shirt to match the suit I was to wear on the programme. When we got to the studios I found that I had left it at the hotel and that the shirt I was wearing did not match the colour of my suit at all. When I asked if I could return to get it, my request was refused. I was not allowed to leave the studios.

Willie John McBride, the captain of the victorious Lions, asked me, 'What size is your collar, Bill?'

'Sixteen and a half.'

'You can borrow mine,' he said. 'It's the colour you'll be needing, the size is OK. It's size nineteen collar.'

It was Willie John, with typical Irish benevolence, who saved the day, but I was thoroughly chastised when I got home, for my wife's keen eyes had spotted the jumbo-size shirt.

There was a great scene of merriment at the bar after the programme, when all the people associated with Gareth gathered together, including the members of the Welsh squad.

Special, memorable invitations like these would unexpectedly be extended to me in the wake of Gareth's success – there were the occasional post-match dinners and gatherings, for example, which I found enjoyable because of their novelty. However, I gathered from more than one wearied reporter that the novelty soon lost its appeal, and that the sameness of faces and conversation took its toll.

The most unexpected invitation was one I received on 3 May 1976 to a dinner at the Royal Sporting Club in London, in honour of Gareth Edwards, MBE. This, one of the greatest accolades a sportsman can receive, was a highlight of his career. It was an impressive occasion; Glan Edwards and I were awed by the palatial surroundings, and by the knowledge that Gareth was the most recent in a very long line of distinguished sportsmen to be thus honoured and the only Welshman ever to receive the distinction.

There were many hundreds of guests there, many of them eminent people, and I was thankful for the anonymous uniformity offered by the formal dress of all present. Sitting at the top table was an unaccustomed, rather unnerving experience, but I soon acclimatised myself to the company. The eloquent speeches in praise of Gareth had a particularly moving effect on both of us, but Gareth's own tribute to his father, which brought loud and deserved applause from all corners of the hall, affected Glan very deeply. At first glance, the occasion could hardly have been more incongruous – a humble Welsh collier the centre of acclaim in a gathering of highly regarded, well-known figures in the Café Royale in London. But to me it seemed a fitting example of the fraternal spirit of sport.

I encountered that fraternal spirit throughout my life: in the enthusiasm of schoolboys, in the generosity of colleagues, in the co-operation of team-work and in the conviviality of social gatherings. I found TV reporters and sports correspondents an indispensable element of the rugby world, and among the most affable.

Chapter Thirteen

Decline and Fall of Welsh Rugby

When I return to the village of Craig-cefn-parc now, I find the change in the area remarkable. The colliery has been bricked off. The Co-op has become a casualty of the entrepreneurial skill of private enterprise. The chapels cannot support a full-time shepherd. What was once marshland is now a park. The chapel vestry has been superseded by a community centre. There is no rugby team, but there are players. Not enough to make a team, so I was told.

I am uncomfortably aware of a general malaise which is spreading through the Welsh society of my boyhood – a change in character, in priorities, in values, which causes me to wonder, sadly, at the way in which we, as Welsh people, have allowed our country to develop, or be developed. According to the County Councils' Association *Jubilee Celebration Book* in 1939, the powerful Glamorgan Labour Council proudly proclaimed the importance of the language 'to develop both national patriotism and national self-respect'. But the language, once so vigorous as our natural medium of communication, is in alarming decline in the Swansea Valley.

I marvel at the fact that such a small nation as Wales has produced so many talented people – Sir Geraint Evans, Philip Madoc, Stuart Burrows, Sian Phillips, Richard Burton, Ryan Davies and Emlyn Williams in the entertainment world, to quote but a few names from a long list of famous Welsh-speaking people. Barry John, Gareth Edwards, Gerald Davies and others have made a significant contribution in the world of rugby. In the world of education and politics the list of well-known and much-respected people is extensive. We belong to a very fine, extremely talented race of people, and our language is our hallmark. It is also our inheritance, and our means of experiencing a whole Welsh way of life. It is a treasure to be respected and enjoyed.

It is at the Arms Park we see the folly of our educational system, which has denied this rich linguistic inheritance to several generations. Passionate men stand proud and erect with their hats or caps in hand, whilst the band and the stadium chorus sing our spine-tingling anthem. Some remain restless, embarrassed, lips tight, unable to express their emotions in song. The Welsh XV stand like Welsh Guardsmen, some singing with fervour, others mumbling, some uncomfortable, others not singing at all. Who is to blame for their ignorance? Is not *Hen Wlad Fy Nhadau* worthy of being taught in our schools?

In my travels I have found a great admiration from fellow Celts and Saxons of the way in which we have retained our language.

'Delighted to hear the Welsh language being used. We teach it here,' said Mr Jack Meyer, headmaster of Millfield.

'We did not get the chance to be bilingual like you,' said the 1950–52 St Luke's students, who came from the anglicised areas of Wales.

The coming of industry into Wales in the last century brought a mixed population of rural Welshmen, Irishmen and West Country men, with the result that some of the Welsh names disappeared from the rugby and soccer teams of Wales. Fenwick, Faulkner, Bennet, Squire, Quinnell, Wheel, Holmes, etc. in rugby, and in soccer Allchurch, Mahoney, Ratcliffe, Rush and Southall are examples of this migration.

We have a gallery of distinguished Welsh sportsmen whose nationality and pride is beyond question, but many of them have never had a real chance to learn the language of their country because the language has been an intrusion in the political circles of Wales. Pride in and a love for one's country are basic needs. I see the demise of the language in many ways in the same terms as the crisis in sport. To lose is honourable, but to lose often, without shape, and to depend on hope is tantamount to a national disgrace. In my opinion, a sense of identity and purpose is important. With it one can venture forward to plan and shape a strong linguistic and sporting destiny; we cannot continue with hit-or-miss schemes.

English people must be the greatest patriots of all. One has only to read Fran Cotton's (England and British Lions) excellent autobiography as an example. I recall one particularly revealing story to illustrate this point. It was told by the captain of the Barbarian rugby team in the post-match dinner at the St Helen's Ground, Swansea, when he announced that he was retiring, having that afternoon played his last match. 'I must impress on you,' he said, 'how proud I am that I was born an Englishman. I was introduced to the game at my prep school. Played for my public school at the Roehampton Sevens. Captained Cambridge University in that epic game in the snow. Joined dear old Rosslyn Park. Played for England at Cardiff in my first international, and captained two Lions tours, one in the Antipodes and the other in South Africa. I am glad I was born an Englishman and played like an Englishman. Now that my rugby days are over, I hope to continue to live, and eventually die, as an Englishman!' From the rear of the hall an unmistakeable Swansea Valley voice was heard: 'Have you *no* ambition, man?'

But there are more than a few Welshmen who would not declare a zeal for their own nation, and who are frequently only too ready to deny their birthright. As good fortune would have it, Evan and his son Berwyn won two grandstand tickets in a raffle for an England v. Wales match at Twickenham, which in those days was held in January. Poor old Evan had looked forward to what he considered was going to be his last trip to HQ. Alas, it did not transpire that way. He developed bronchitis due to excessive inhalation of coal dust. 'Take my ticket down to the club, and sell it for the same price as we paid for it, Berwyn,' said Evan, with a tinge of regret. Berwyn had no difficulty in selling to a club member, whose gratitude was beyond measure. 'For my son, Idwal. He's a doctor in London, you know.'

When the big day came, Berwyn, slightly under the weather, sat pensively in the stand. He saw Idwal, dressed like a tailor's dummy, a few rows ahead of him. 'He's too posh for me!' muttered Berwyn to himself.

The game started with Wales kicking into a very stiff breeze. 'Well done, Wales!' shouted Berwyn, but his praise turned to despair as the English full-back fielded a very awkward ball and with a torpedo-kick sent the ball soaring into the sky, over the Welsh twenty-five and near the touchline, to roll forward to hit the corner flag and bounce into touch. Berwyn was struck dumb by such perfect execution. His heart fluttered with the danger resulting from that kick. His dismay paled into insignificance, though, when he saw Idwal standing on his feet in great ecstasy, shouting with glee, 'Come on, England! Well done, chaps.'

And yet, I believe that the days are gone when Welshmen are ashamed to be Welsh. The sense of inferiority from which they suffered is no longer evident. But they still lack confidence in themselves.

At this moment there is a lack of confidence in Welsh rugby too. Not only does the game change, but men do. We must forget what happened yesterday and plan for tomorrow, now. Many of those who basked in the glory of coaching publicly abuse it now. I find that reaction disturbing. It must be remembered that only great players can make modest coaches great.

There seems to be a head-in-the-sand attitude; we refuse to learn from others. The WRU seem oblivious to the fact that other nations are leaving us behind. New Zealand in 1971 and South Africa in 1974 humbly declared that they had learnt something from the Lions' visits. To their credit, they revised their concepts and regained the ascendancy, for in their humility they were prepared to learn from those who were better. To know everything is to know nothing.

Many new expedients have been tried in the '80s to halt the ignominy of Wales losing too often. Players, captains, coaches and selectors have been changed. But one factor has *not* been changed, and that is the method or style of play which matches our mental and physical characteristics as Welshmen. We are too small in physique to use bulldozer methods, for we are a breed of whippets, corgies and sheepdogs. We are the subtle of hand and the deft of foot, and the sooner we revert to playing with brains, and not brawn, the sooner we will be able to bask in the sunshine of rugby success. There is no doubt that Wales possesses the talent. The bad results of recent years have produced frustrations and acrimony, or we would not have allowed the likes of Jeff Squire, Graham Price, Gareth Davies and David Richards to go out through the back door of Welsh rugby. They had served Wales with pride and dignity and their retirement should have been acknowledged in a way befitting their great service to Wales. In no way should our heroes sneak out of the international arena without a visible token of thanks from the WRU.

If Wales wanted to be superior in sport, rugby in particular, there would have to be a national physical education programme in our schools whereby, after a certain age, specialisation would begin, and every step thereafter would be monitored to ensure that progress continued until maturity.

England's philosophy towards raising standards in sport is by providing monolithic sports centres. They have become the haven of the middle-class at the expense of the lower social group, whose prime contact with the centres is to daub them with graffiti or vandalise them. A Welsh Parliament, perhaps, could decree that all children should be educated to use sports-centre facilities during their stay in school. What is important is that we in Wales aim high.

It would be a wonderful step forward if the post of director of physical education – a real, accountable post, not a sinecure, like so many of the administrative posts in Wales today – could be established in every one of the eight Welsh counties. The holder of the post would be responsible for monitoring the development of sport for all age groups and social classes.

There is nothing to prevent us producing real world-class champions in all facets of sport. New Zealand's population is slightly larger than that of Wales. They can, with great confidence, compete with the rest of the world with a measure of success in *every* international sport. In 1984, and in England in 1986, they even took Test series against England in cricket. Wales could and should emulate New Zealand, even transcend their achievements, for we happen to live in a part of the world where international competition is more available.

Rugby is our national game, and yet our pride in it has taken some hard knocks in recent years. Things reached such a pass that a sub-committee was formed to look into the state of the game in Wales. Within a few days of the announcement of the sub-committee, a prominent member of it asked me if I would write down any thoughts I had on the matter. I refused, because the sub-committee was composed entirely of dedicated disciples of coaching, whereas a balance of members whose thoughts were not in total agreement with coaching would, in my view, have been more productive. This book is my contribution. It chronicles the thoughts, many of them controversial both at their time and in the present climate, which I have formulated during my many years of teaching, coaching, supporting, nurturing and enjoying a game which always has been, and always will be, at the core of my Welshness. It is to the future of Welsh rugby football that I dedicate these thoughts.

Epilogue

The Changing Face of Rugby

The deep depression which followed the halcyon days of 1969–79 is still over us in 1998. How was it that little Wales, with a population the size of Greater Manchester, managed what now seems to have been a miracle, not only in rugby, but in all other major sports as well? The credit must go to the Board of Education, who had the brainwave of equipping all secondary schools with three-year-trained specialist PE teachers. These young men and women awoke in boys and girls previously slumbering abilities, significantly altered their behaviour and attitudes and accomplished the metamorphosis that led to Welsh rugby's golden years.

Ineptitude was transformed into that supreme competence that allows flair to flourish. The young saw visions and the old dreamed dreams. Success in sport created a new, proud awareness of nationhood. No longer was it the names of the kings and queens of England that were learnt by heart in schoolrooms, but the names and jersey-numbers of the squad. And pride in Welsh achievements on the rugby field led to a desire to know more about the history of Gwalia fach.

Those stars of the great period who had any aptitude for public speaking were fêted at rugby dinners all over the UK and well rewarded for their contributions. They naturally included in their speeches stories with a local flavour, such as the story of Hywel and Glen.

Hywel and Glen were regular and popular customers at their local, Y Brew. In those days, stop-tap was ten o'clock, with half an hour's extension on special occasions such as bank holidays. It was

Christmas, and the two friends were just getting comfortably merry when a loud voice intruded: 'Time, gentlemen, please!'

This familiar problem was easily solved: they took a taxi to the small coal-mining town of Ammanford, where the night club was loud with seasonal music and the cheerful voices of irrepressibly buoyant merrymakers. The door was bolted, of course. Glen knocked vigorously and after a while a tired, wheezing retired collier reluctantly arrived, opened the door a crack and said, 'You can't come in 'ere. Past closing time.'

'Aw, come on.'

'You can't come in 'ere. Final, that is. Rules is rules,' coughed the old collier, his chest raw with the smoke of his Woodbine. All his life he had been powerless; now he had sway over the opening and shutting of that door, and he was not going to relinquish it.

'Aw, come on, man,' coaxed Glen. 'Spirit of Christmas, eh? Don't you recognise my friend here?'

'No, I don't. Who is 'e, then?'

'Hywel Bennett, of course. Star of stage, screen and television.'

'I don' care if 'e's Phil Bennett, he's not coming in 'ere after stop-tap! And that's for sure.' And the door closed, and that was the end of Christmas cheer for Hywel and Glen.

Phil Bennett spent his rugby career playing for the renowned Llanelli RFC, where the 'sospans' on the goalposts are a reminder that the town was once famous for its tin- and steel-works. And of Llanelli's other claim to fame – the ditty 'Sospan fach', which is sung at rugby clubs all over the world. There is a particularly Welsh atmosphere at Stradey Park because the club's supporters come not only from the town, but the surrounding rural areas of West Wales where people speak Welsh and English with equal facility. These supporters are always enthusiastic, but in Phil Bennett's prime it is not unfair to say that they were fanatical.

It happened that, at the height of the enthusiasm of the '70s, with Wales in the international limelight and the whole town crazy with rugby fever, the town council found it necessary to advertise for an additional groundsman. The deluge of applications was, eventually, reduced to a short-list of three, and it was a source of some pride to the council that it had avoided parochialism by naming a Welshman, an Irishman and an Asian.

A special committee was appointed to interview the candidates, and when it convened the chairman said, 'As you can clearly see, gentlemen, from the short-list, we have been scrupulously fair. Furthermore, I have devised a simple system: I shall ask each applicant one question only, and from his answer it will be for you to decide the best man for the job.'

The Welshman was interviewed first. 'When was the investiture of Charles as Prince of Wales?' the chairman asked him. 'Easy!' he replied, and answered quite correctly, as did the Irishman when asked, 'What colour are the Mountains of Mourne?' The Asian now entered. 'Who was the hooker who played for Llanelli during the season 1923–24?' 'I'm sorry, sir, I have no idea.' The committee could not believe their ears.

Although Welsh rugby was on the crest of the wave, it was humbled by a nation almost as small as itself – Seland Newydd. The All Blacks are the team we (Llanelli especially!) like to beat, but the last time Wales beat them was in 1953. Since then they have developed their game to a point where we have no chance whatsoever against them, away or at home. How is it that a nation of only 3.3 million people can lead the world as they do today?

Their population is indeed small, but their rugby-playing population is not. New Zealand has 1,000 clubs and 100,000 players; Wales has 440 clubs and 25,000 players. What's more, New Zealand are not averse to including the occasional Samoan and Fijian in their ranks in order to retain their dominance.

Three years ago I visited Fiji, Australia and New Zealand, and in New Zealand I attended an Under-Fifteen match. The two teams were ill-matched, but the better team had no compunction about piling on the points: they showed just as much enthusiasm when they scored their seventieth point as they had when they scored their first try. These schoolboys never smiled; they were tough and strong, rugby was for them a deeply serious business and winning was everything. I visited a number of schools and, if they were typical, there is no such thing as the Corinthian ideal in New Zealand. And the women are just as competitive in their sports as the men. In New Zealand 'Sport for all' is a reality, not a slogan.

During Wales's great period, the WRU made the fundamental mistake of being complacent. But, as an international referee put it,

'Once Gareth Edwards put his tools in the bar, Welsh rugby lost its grip.' When the Union began to realise its mistake, think-tanks were set up – but talk is easy and the solution is not. English-born players were brought in, a move that must have had the heroes of old turning in their graves. Wales continued to be out-thought, out-conditioned and out-played, not only by the giants of the rugby world but by its dwarfs as well. Strange new theories were applied which discouraged the innate running genius of the Welsh and replaced it with tactics which on occasion turned their play into something between a cattle stampede and a flock of chickens scratching in a barnyard. Wales became a regular candidate for the wooden spoon!

One has to commiserate with those who have played for their country during the last two decades – but it is hardly credible that so many of them were coached regularly from the age of eight, and yet, at the age of twenty-eight, could not be relied upon to field a high ball, find touch and avoid getting injured in tackles. The truth is that the WRU failed to recognise soon enough that a revolution had occurred under their very noses. It did not take a genius to see that what distinguished the players of the golden era was that, in addition to being strong, fast, flexible, skilled and durable, they could catch, pass, throw, kick, dribble and tackle – in short, they were past masters of the basics.

In Wales at that time, we had PE teachers in the schools who had played at a high level and were qualified and experienced in teaching and coaching at all levels: Hywel Thomas (Llanelli Grammar School, sevens expert; county adviser in PE; former chairman of Llanelli RFC), Goronwy Morgan (Llandovery College, sevens expert and rugby innovator), Roy Bish (Neath Grammar School, St Luke's College and Cyncoed lecturer; Italian national coach; Cardiff RFC), John Harries (Bassaleg CS, mentor of Stuart Barnes and Jon Callard). And a knowledgeable journalist such as Stephen Jones of *The Sunday Times*. Why were they never asked to help? They would not have permitted Wales to sink to such depths.

Disraeli said that the youth of the nation are the trustees of its posterity. When a Secretary of State for Education officially downgrades PE in the curriculum he is condemning the country to mediocrity in sport. What happens at the Arms Park is a direct consequence of what happens – or fails to happen – in Welsh schools.

Participation in a full programme of PE ought to be statutory. No amount of blanket-coaching thereafter can make up for neglect during the formative years, even if the coaches were good – and they are not. Today any Tom, Dick or Harry with a teaspoonful of rugby knowledge can become a coach or top administrator. Mediocrities breeding mediocrity.

When Gareth Edwards had a trial with Swansea Valley schoolboys (Under-Fifteen) at centre, he was taken off for his own safety by a wise schoolmaster who felt that he was too small to survive. He had tasted rejection, and it was a serious blow to his pride, especially as some of his classmates had been chosen. I had discovered, however, that the Valley XV were struggling to find a scrum-half, and stayed behind after school to teach him the rudiments of the position. Within a month he was a regular member of the team, his self-respect restored by a taste of local fame.

He *was* small – five feet three inches and eight stone five – so I was careful to give attention to his speed, strength, suppleness, agility and stamina as well as his skills. This was essential if he was to avoid serious injury in a physical game which can at any moment become violent. I soon began to delight in teaching him, for he was as absorbent as a sponge and possessed a rare gift of self-correction. A word to the wise was always enough. 'Success only comes from repetition, Gareth,' I would say. 'I can't train for you. You've got to do that for yourself.'

In the gym and on the playing-fields with the other boys he demonstrated a will to win and, in contrast to his effervescent nature, the killer instinct of the supreme competitor. In summer the emphasis was on athletics and here Gareth's versatility was a problem. To my mind he lacked the pace of a sprinter, was too small to make a top-class thrower and too short for a jumper – yet he had a cabinet full of trophies to prove me wrong. I decided to make a hurdler of him because of the affinity between that and rugby. Primitive beginnings using makshift hurdles led, when he was at Millfield (no shortage of hurdles there), to his becoming record-breaking champion of Wales and of England as well. While at Pontardawe Tech he was nominated most promising young athlete in Wales. Such successes provided the motivation he needed, the motivation for hard work and yet more hard work, for it was this, more than his talents, that made him. His admirers will always remember those explosive starts and surging runs in rugby grounds all over the world. He became tough-minded and highly competitive at the highest level – and never, in the whole of his playing career, sustained a serious injury. Yet there were WRU coaches, ex-internationals among them, who, dizzy with their eminence and forgetful of the maxim that it is the quality of the player that makes the coach great, not vice versa, did not rate him. 'Know-how' of this quality is what made Welsh rugby small.

I have deliberately reminded the reader of Gareth's beginnings at this point because I wish to emphasise the connection between his phenomenal success and the status of PE in our schools. Did Gareth's classmates stand around admiring his achievements? Of course not: they made every effort to emulate them and as a result improved their own performance.

I first saw Jonathan Davies, virtually unknown at that time, in a match between Neath and Llanelli in the early '80s and was struck, and entertained, by his chameleon behaviour: he was, in turn, cocky, impishly humorous and even arrogant. He evidently intended to prove to everyone watching, whether on TV or at the ground, that Jonathan Davies had arrived – and in doing so he demonstrated touches of genius.

For example, standing casually on the twenty-two-metre line with the ball in his hands ready for a drop-out, quick as a flash he tapped it over the line, picked it up, shot up the field and passed to Neath's British Lion, Elgan Rees, for a try that clinched the match 31–29. Jonathan put a smile on the face of everyone who saw him play and was instantly recognised as Welsh rugby's new Messiah.

The next time I saw him was at a dinner where he and Paul Thorburn were guest speakers. Both, by now, were in the celebrity bracket, modest young internationals who could speak entertainingly and without resort to the kind of Billingsgate language that so often passes for humour these days. A necessary part of genius is respect for decorum and the traditions of a great game.

When dinner was over the guests intermingled freely and, inevitably, conversation turned to the icons of the early '70s. The immortals were showered with praise and the two current stars relegated – a sad business, I thought – to the role of listeners. Later, when I was introduced to them, we had an interesting technical discussion about covering and defending, in particular the central importance of half- and full-backs being able to kick with either foot. They were two fine young players, but two, three, even four such players do not make a team capable of winning a World Cup – as Jonathan and Paul dejectedly discovered in 1987.

The WRU, as usual, was not to blame. Its members claimed, indeed, that defeating Australia 22–21 made Wales third in the world rankings – an allegation shatteringly refuted by the semi-final score (Wales 6, New Zealand 49) and on the subsequent tour, when New Zealand scored 106 points in two matches against Wales's 12. Yet eminent ex-internationals had predicted that Wales would *win* the series. As the Welsh proverb has it, 'Long tongue, little knowledge'. Jonathan was the only player who returned from New Zealand with his reputation enhanced, and he alone was thought worthy of inclusion in an All Black XV.

Other players might have been delighted with this accolade, but Jonathan regarded the tour as an unmitigated disaster. The whole team, in his view, himself included, had let their country down. He tried to get a meeting with the WRU to discuss how the game in Wales might be reshaped and revitalised. And they rejected him, with a mixture of incredulity and anger, as a cheeky young whipper-snapper. Whatever next!

He played his last game for his country against Romania in 1988 and naturally got the blame for what was considered a débâcle. All afternoon the Romanian captain, fly-half Gelu Ignat, directed prodigious kicks deep into the Welsh half, and Jonathan, out of sorts on the day, failed to work the miracles which Wales expects these days, no longer from the team, but from its few individuals of genius.

His unsatisfactory relationship with the WRU showed no signs of improving. Like most of us, he wanted to be liked; like all good players, he expected to enjoy the game. Failure is a success if you can learn from it, though. He was offered, by manager Doug Laughton, a deal with Widnes which he could not turn down and he signed for them, although his heart remained always in Wales. The WRU had blundered again. Not their fault, of course!

When I met Jonathan again it was in a most unconventional manner. My elder son, Rhodri, became acquainted in British Columbia with Mike Nicholas, former Aberafan, Warrington and

Wales star, while Mike was touring with the London Welsh Veterans. When he learned that Rhodri would be home in Wales for Christmas, he invited him to be his guest for a few days and watch the Boxing Day derby match between Widnes and Warrington. 'Bring your Dad with you,' he said. 'He'll enjoy seeing Jonathan again.'

We spent some very pleasant hours with Mike and Jonathan. Their conversation was fascinating, and we were allowed into the inner sanctums of the club where the facilities, social as well as rugby, are admirable. What impressed me most was the discipline of the league game, which reminded me at once of those schoolboys in New Zealand. Even off the field, the professional players were grim and unsmiling, their thoughts concentrated on the impending game and how to win it.

Rugby league is tough, tougher by far than union at that time. We stayed on in the clubhouse after the match, to savour the atmosphere. Widnes had defeated their rivals, but there was no hilarity, only a grave kind of satisfaction. Jonathan had been sitting with us for some time, wrapped up like his colleagues in his own thoughts, his half-pint glass empty. 'Let me buy you a drink,' I ventured.

'No, thanks,' he replied, politely.

'Come on, Jonathan, you've earned it after a tough match like that.'

'If I'd been playing for Neath,' he said, with a glance at his watch, 'I'd be on my fourth pint by now. But I'm so weary I doubt if I could lift a pint glass.' Three hours later we joined him, his lovely wife Karen and a few close friends for a splendid dinner in a country-house hotel. The Welsh couple were enthusiastic about the kindness with which they had been received in the north-west – although at the same time there was the inevitable touch of hiraeth for home. Before the evening was over, Jonathan boldly asserted that he was going to end his career by returning to Wales to play rugby union again. 'I've set my heart on it,' he insisted.

Some hope, I thought at the time. The WRU had never, to my knowledge, forgiven any transgressor of the Rubicon between the 'amateur' and the professional game. I can think of only one player, Glyn John of Leigh, St Luke's College and, in 1954, Wales, sadly dead now, who was reinstated, and that was because he had signed forms for Leigh before reaching the age of eighteen. But Jonathan's confidence was entirely justified: he returned triumphantly home to a Wales that had never rejected him, truly the conquering hero. And played some fine games until Father Time caught up with him.

He had no part in the disgraceful 1991 tour to Australia, when the post-match events at Ballymore in Brisbane made a nonsense of the idea of pride in representing one's country. The boorish behaviour on that occasion caused people back home to hide their heads in shame. Wales were inept on the pitch and disgraced off it by a band of anti-social louts unworthy, in any case, of their caps. Am I hopelessly old-fashioned in these graceless days to believe that players representing the country abroad are ambassadors, and by their conduct the rest of us will be judged? Never again must we send abroad players devoid of discipline, and managers, selectors and administrators incapable of giving the necessary leadership and unconcerned about their own incompetence. Bad preparation leads to worse teams which leads to appalling behaviour; discipline and good coaching lead to team spirit, high morale, self-confidence, good humour, clean hard play on the field and good friendships off it.

Wales was in despair until a coup as unlikely as the destruction of the Berlin Wall and the conversion of the USSR occurred: a group of solicitors forced the WRU to capitulate. Grandiose schemes were brought forward. No need now for the surreptitious brown envelope: players became professional, money an acceptable reward. 'Wales for the World Cup' was the cry. And three leagues, Sky Television, a new national stadium, and sponsorship *sans frontières*.

Of all these, money was the greatest, but with it came squabbling, breakaways, expulsions and greed. These were the words that filled the newspapers' rugby columns. Welsh supporters, in spite of their propensity to argue over anything and everything, were supportive in principle of anything that might make Welsh rugby great again. The true supporter is not much interested in ways and means: he or she has one priority, and only one – a team. Youngsters at school need players of flair to copy, to aspire to, and Wales needs a national XV that will make the nation proud. Hundreds of thousands of supporters have been lost because the 'reformed' WRU has been no more successful than its discredited predecessor in finding creative coaches with the vision to discover and develop players of supreme skill and high morale. 'Winning isn't everything.' Don't you believe it!

The damage can be seen at its worst at school level. School pitches catch the eye these days – because nobody is playing on them. One famous Welsh rugby school finds it hard to field even a First XV. Once upon a time Cwmtawe School had forty – yes, forty – staff members willing to give up their spare time to help with inter-school matches. That kind of goodwill and *esprit de corps* has been sacrificed on the altar of 'higher standards' and 'failing teachers'.

The other day, in Cwmgors, I met an athletic-looking boy striding sturdily along the pavement. He wore a black tracksuit and black runners, on his head was a black cap, and underneath his arm was a brown-paper parcel. I jumped to the (for me) obvious conclusion. 'Going to play rugby, are you?' I asked, in Welsh. He was obviously nonplussed, so I repeated the question in English. 'Don't be daft,' he said. 'I'm going to change my video.'

What are we to do when a recent survey shows that sixty per cent of our sixteen-year-olds take no formal physical exercise at all? While public schools devote at least ten hours a week to games, state schools are lucky if they can manage two. Trained specialist PE teachers are required to instil the basics of any game, but rugby needs their skills more than most. Who wants devolution? I do – if it means an end to the present shambles they call PE and the establishment of a real Welsh schools system tailored to the real needs of Wales. Mr Peter Hain MP, the Welsh Minister of Education, or his successor can be the saviour of Welsh sport, for it is he who has the power to change. May I remind you of Disraeli's words. We ignore our youth at our peril.

My advice to Gareth Edwards seems awfully naive today. We have megastars now, and the worldly wise advice to them is, 'Travel alone, lad. Sponsors will be more generous if they see the product by itself. The presence of others distracts their attention.' After a game at Llanelli I observed a Welsh megastar approached by a smiling daughter of the East. Would he be so very kind as to step outside so that she could take a few photographs? Yes, he would – and a few moments later he was back, with an extremely expensive camera tucked under his arm.

We have always recognised in Wales that rugby is the people's game. The thin, the fat, the weak, the slow – all of them are welcome so long as they have rugby in their hearts. There is a special affinity between rugby and the Welsh nation, and the Corinthian philosophy was an important part of that affinity.

The Rugby Football Union was formed in 1871, but unity was lost in 1895 when the Northern Union (later the Rugby League) split from it. The disagreement was one of principle: Union favoured the status quo; Northern Union wanted 'broken time' payments to compensate for loss of Saturday earnings.

The RFU continued to maintain, officially at least, that rugby was played for enjoyment; their ideal was the Corinthians. The great London clubs – Quins, Wasps, Richmond, Blackheath and Rosslyn Park – never wavered from the Corinthian ideal.

Llanelli RFC came into existence in 1872 and, with the aid of the pennies of its exuberant supporters – steelworkers, colliers, farmers – established a glowing reputation. When I became a regular member of the team, I became the recipient of the brown envelope mentioned earlier, and the WRU member turned a blind eye. All the club's officers were honorary (treasurer, chairman, secretary), as were all the members of its committee, and they received no payment for their work. When the RFU declared the game open, shockwaves shook the land, amplified when people learned that the London bastions had not merely fallen, but were first in the queue for the shekels with which to scour the world for talent.

Changes in the laws made the union game more attractive to its audience and the stars of rugby league found their lustre dimmed. Their status up north counted for little down south and the union players espoused the philosophy of the Snowdonian shepherd and kept their gates closed. Suddenly what the northerners had always dismissed as a soft game became a hunting-ground for tigers.

Llanelli were more optimistic than most about the possibilities of a professional game. They quickly found a sponsor, a consortium was set up and their future seemed secure. People unaccustomed to business ethics often suppose that a binding agreement can be secured by the shaking of hands, overlooking the well-known fact that those who have acquired the most wealth are often the most reluctant to part with even a little of it. That, after all, is how they became rich in the first place. 'What's in it for me?' they enquire.

Llanelli's consortium collapsed and the club was left with no alternative but to sell its assets to the WRU with an understanding that when it regained solvency it would be permitted to buy back Stradey Park. The *Llanelli Star* published details of the salaries of the non-playing staff: Director of Coaching, £50,000; Chief Executive, £45,000; Player-Coach, £40,000; Team Manager, £20,000; Financial Directors (2), £20,000 and £15,000 respectively; Administrative Assistant, £12,000; Shop Manager, undisclosed; total £202,000 plus.

Such was the club's self-confidence that Frano Botica (New Zealand and Wigan), class player and ace-kicker, was signed up. In order to transfer him it was necessary to pay Castleford £150,000, Orrell £150,000, Frano £150,000 and two 'bonuses' of £50,000 – total £550,000. As the *Western Mail* said, that was the kind of mistake that can only lead to the wall.

Until quite recently there was harmony in Welsh rugby, even if we played it badly. Now that the professional game has been foisted upon us, the ethics of the game have become irrelevant. Players are employees now, to be hired and fired at will; to do as they are told, or else; to succeed or lose their livelihood. A World Cup player told me that being picked for the World Cup is not a great honour, but 'boring beyond belief'. Playing the matches is fine, but the dreary hanging on, allied to monotonous training schedules, becomes soul-destroying. Especially when you know that there are only three real contenders – South Africa, Australia and New Zealand – with England and France, at best, good outsiders, and Wales . . .

The professional player has to be groomed to extract the maximum amount of money from the game while he can by promoting himself through exhibition matches, public appearances and TV shows. He will feign injury in a televised match so as to get the cameras focused on his sponsors' logos. The Gareth Edwardses and Jonathan Davieses of today do not play for their countries, but for Gilbert, Adidas or Nike. They have so much time on their hands that training becomes mere hard work; they cannot become naturally fit like the amateurs who earned their living by manual work, but develop balloon-muscles more suited to the beach than the pitch. The availability of performance-enhancing drugs has already – inevitably – become a serious temptation. With commercial inducements to perform, and financial sanctions if one fails to do so, anything that might rapidly make one faster, stronger and more aggressive is hard to resist.

The club rugby coach has become more accountable and much

more subject to pressure. It is a lonely job at best – one cannot succeed without talented players, of whom there is always a shortage (and it is much worse now that the few real talents can be cornered by the highest bidder). A coach rides a roller-coaster: briefly elated when his players succeed, deeply depressed, and harassed by the media, when they fail. Team coaching in the UK is the worst in the world and nobody, it seems, is prepared to do anything constructive about it. Mediocrity in sport is sport's own fault: hundreds of well-paid sinecures have been created in administration and the combined efforts of their holders, particularly in team sports, have produced lamentable results.

The much-maligned referee, however, is at last about to command respect and receive payment commensurate with his skills and the pressure he is under – particularly with increased media coverage – to stamp out intimidation, dissent, ill manners and aggression. If the game is to flourish and to be played in its true spirit, dirty and dangerous play must be got rid of.

It is sad to see so many of the great players of the past now troubled with arthritis and rheumatism. Even the immortal Bleddyn Williams has had to have two knee operations. It disturbs me to see former stars with 'disabled' discs on the windscreens of their cars, a former international prop unable to turn his head freely or a former full-back wince with pain when he kicks a football for his grandson. Yet these players never trained with half the intensity required of modern professionals. What kind of a middle age are they creating for themselves? We need to protect our best players from the excessive training demanded by over-ambitious clubs.

I remain a devout lover of the amateur game which served so many of us so well. It is depressing to see a game that enriched our lives, creating entertainment and good fellowship, demeaned by the demands of mere money, to see daggers drawn and tempers frayed. I have such glowing memories of the game I knew, a players' game. I feel deeply obliged, also, to the game that opened the door for me to become a teacher, introduced me to people I would not otherwise have met and gave me such opportunities and such good fortune. Next only to family and friends, rugby has been the most important thing in my life.

In my day the game *was* a game: you won some, you lost some;

there was no slavery to a sponsor interested in success for gain's, not fulfilment's, sake. To lose an important match today is to sin against the Holy Ghost; to turn the other cheek is unprofessional; to play foul for professional reasons, praiseworthy. What should be disciplined fun has become mere discipline, a chore. When a game is a game no longer, and players cease to delight in performance for its own sake and the sake of their self-respect, it is doomed because it has degenerated from a human activity to a mechanical one.

I should dearly love to live to see Welsh rugby great again. With devolution I believe that there is a chance. But we need to start again from the grass-roots, making sure, first of all, that our children get a fair deal in every aspect of physical education. *Mens sana in corpore sano*, Juvenal wrote, 'a healthy mind in a healthy body'. I am not at all sure that the national curriculum, school league tables and the pursuit of 'higher standards' in education are going to give our children healthy minds; I am sure that the demotion of physical education, especially team games, has already deprived many children of healthy bodies. And we need to find some way, at club level, of combining what was best in the Corinthian ideal with a true professionalism.

As I write these final words, I recognise that the time of writing, June 1998, stands out not only for its incessant rain, but also for the woeful rugby performances of the home nations against teams in the southern hemisphere, as well as far from satisfactory results in the soccer World Cup and, of course, in cricket.

Having promised a new approach to the teaching of physical education in schools, New Labour must not be afraid of change. It is the only thing that brings progress.

If we carry on as we are now, our annual performances against the major foreign countries will continue to be lamentable, and only school PE can change that. The new millennium provides us with a challenge. For the sake of our children and our grandchildren, let us take it on.

Envoi

God's Hall of Fame

To have your name up there is greater yet by far
Than all the halls of fame down here, and every man a star.
This crowd on earth they soon forget the heroes of the past,
They cheer like mad until you fall, and that's how long you last.

I tell you, friends, I would not trade my name, however small,
If written there beyond the stars in that celestial hall,
For any famous man on earth, or glory that they share:
I'd rather be an unknown here, and have my name up there.

ANON

Index

Aaron, Sid 76
Aberavon RFC 145
Allchurch, Ivor 138
Amman United RFC 51, 63, 66
Athletics 94
Australia 177, 179

Barnes, Stuart 174
Barran, Max 132
Bebb, Dewi 128
Bennett, Hywel 171–2
Bennett, Phil 34, 135, 160, 172
Bevan, John (Welsh wing three-quarter) 136
Bevan, John (Welsh outside-half) 160
Bignal, Mary 107
Bish, Roy 174
Board of Education brings PE to schools 171
Botica, Frano 182
Bowen, Bleddyn 148
Bowes, Stan 124
Boxing 24
Boyce, Max 84

Brace, Onllwyn 96, 147, 155, 160
Brooke, Zin Zan 147
Broughton Rovers RLC 66

Callard, Jon 174
Campese, David 147
Cardiff City FC 43, 45
Cardiff College of Education 76
Cardiff RFC 42, 60, 77, 79, 119, 121, 124
Carnegie College 136
Charles, John 143
Clydach Merthyr Colliery 36, 47, 48
'Corinthians' 61, 141, 173, 184
Cotton, Fran 135, 167
Cullen, Matt 95
Cwmtawe School 146

Daniel, Bobby 38
Davey, Claude 82–3, 147
Davies, Brychan 137
Davies, David ('Dai Cender') 65–8
Davies, Dr Elwyn 158
Davies, Gareth 147, 168

Davies, Geoff 141
Davies, Gerald 133, 136, 145, 160, 165
Davies, Gordon 137
Davies, Gwynfor 139
Davies, Hugh 139
Davies, Huw Llewellyn 99
Davies, John Duncan 147
Davies, Jonathan 147, 176–8
Davies, Lyn 137
Davies, Mervyn 119, 145, 160
'Death-Ray Stars' 33–5, 45
Dispensation Law 130
Duckham, David 160

Edwards, Gareth 88 enters Pontardawe Boys' Secondary Technical School; 90 scrum-half for Swansea Valley Schools XV; 91 gymnast; 92–4 athlete; 94 Under-Fifteen trials, County Champion; 95 Welsh Secondary Schools trial; 96 kicking; 98 soccer; 98 hooker; 100 polevaulter; 100 hurdler; 100 Under-Nineteen trial; 102 with Barry John; 102 Glamorgan County XV; 103–4 breaking Welsh hurdles record; 104 'Most Promising Athlete'; 105 early achievements; 107–18 at Millfield; 118 British Schools hurdles champion; 119 at Cardiff College of Education; 121 Cardiff RFC trials; 127 first cap; 128 against England; 129 passing; 131–2 individual try against Scotland, Lions tour of New Zealand; 133–4 loses interest in rugby; 157–9 speeches; 160 charity matches; 160 opinion of outside-halfs; 161–4 This Is Your Life; 164 MBE; 174 Wales loses grip
Edwards, Gethin 141
Edwards, Glan 93, 98, 103, 115, 127–8, 157, 164
Edwards, Horace 70
Edwards, Mrs Annie 93, 98, 108, 115, 127–8
Evans, Emrys 68
Evans, Gwyn 50
Evans, Ieuan 152
Evans, Ken 139

Fallowfield, Bill 65
Ford, Trevor 38
Forward, Alan 142
France, College Tour 74–5

Gaunt, Marilyn (This Is Your Life) 161, 163
Glais RFC 50, 69
Glamorgan, County 94 athletics; 137–8 PE became compulsory subject
God's Hall of Fame 185
Going, Sid 131
Griffiths, Dr John 141
Gwaen-cae-gurwen Youth Centre 95

Hain, Peter 180
Halifax RLC 68
Hallesey, Harry 161
Harries, Ronnie 46

Hicks, Cyril 45
Hill, Sid 116
Hopkin, Jeff 139
Hopkin, Phil 79
Hopkin, William John 43
Hughes, Bill 68
Hullin, Billy 122

Ignat, Gelu 177

James, Carwyn 142–3, 147
James, Les 96
James, Ron 86
Jarrett, Keith 128
Jenkins, Albert 122
Jenkins, Brice 78
Jenkins, Neil 62
Jenkins, Trevor 92
John, Barry 34, 102, 145, 147, 160, 129, 130, 133, 165
John, David 96–7
John, Glyn 178
John, J.H. 27–35
Jones, Bill Erith 139
Jones, Dan 54–6
Jones, Danny 43
Jones, Ken 119, 147
Jones, Lewis 147
Jones, McLeod 139
Jones, Moelwyn 46
Jones, Robert 148
Jones, Stephen 174
Jones, Winston 157
Joseph, Wyn 139

Kelleher, Jeff 149

Laidlaw, Chris 131

Lewis, Gwyn 141
Lewis, Tony 134
Lewis, Wayne 117
Llanelli RFC 58, 61–2, 69, 145, 172, 181
Loughborough College 136

McBride, Willie John 163
McCandless, Billy 43–4
Manfield, Ron 59
Martin, Alan 143, 145, 160
Mathews, Grindell 31
Meads, Colin 91
Meredith, Bryn 74
Meyer, R.J.O. 107, 114–5, 119, 166
Millfield School 107, 114, 117, 175
Morgan, Cliff 34, 77
Morgan, Goronwy 74, 96, 155, 174
Morgan, John 101, 139, 140
Morris, Dai 160
Morris, Trevor 43

Neath RFC 66, 178
New Zealand 131–2, 135, 168–9, 173, 177
Nicholas, Mike 177

Oldham RLC 67

Phillips, Horace 50
Physical education 91 at Pontardawe; 136–7, 141–2, 145–6 effects of comprehensive reorganisation; 154 in 'Better Schools'; 169 national policy for PE
Pickering, Ron 100
Pontardawe Golf Club 100
Pontardawe Grammar School 140

Pontardawe RFC 46, 79

Pontardawe 'Tech' (Boys' Secondary Technical School and College of Further Education, later Cwmtawe Comprehensive School) 42–3, 79

Porter, Gwyn 122–4

Price, David 119

Price, David John 36

Price, Graham, 168

Reed, Jeff 139

Rees, Bilo 63–6

Rees, David 137

Rees, Elgan 176

Referee 183

Richards, David 168

Richards, Maurice 145

Romania 177

Rugby League Football 181

Rugby Union Football 19 versus soccer; 28 miners' interest in; 29 advice on positions; 45 effect of War upon; 42 freemasonry of; 53 West Country and; 92–3 coaching and athletics; 95 brotherhood of; 125 'perks' of; 127 in the doldrums; 133 coaching; 136 the '70s; 137 character building; 138–9 contribution of schoolmasters to; 139 'Ten Commandments of rugby; 142 and drinking; 143 changes; 143 aggression in; 145 coaching outside of school; 146 effect of small and large schools; 148 loss of monopoly; 150 early specialisation; 151 'psyching up'; 152 altered attitudes to; 152 small communities and; 154 schoolboys' or club?; 155 coaches and coaching; 160 charity matches; 167 patriotism

St Luke's College 68–9, 75–6, 136

Samuel, Gary 122

Samuel, Iestyn 133

Samuel, Rhodri 177–8

Scott, Bob 68

Second World War 45, 49

Secretary of State downgrades PE in schools 174

Smeall, James, MA 69–70

Soccer 16–17, 37, 39

South Africa 168

Sparrow, Eric 71–2

Spencer, John 160

Sponsors 110

Squire, Jeff 168

Sullivan, Jim 66

Sutton, Roy 96

Swansea RFC 27, 51, 119

Swansea Valley 80–1, 147, 160

Swinton RLC 63, 139

Tanner, Haydn 78, 96, 147

Taylor, John 133

Technical Education 146

'Terrible Eight' 122

Thomas, Arwel 148

Thomas, Delme 143

Thomas, Eric 76

Thomas, Gareth 139

Thomas, Greg 148

Thomas, Harry 74

Thomas, Hywel 174

Thomas, Oswald, OBE, MSc 80–1, 85, 116
Thorburn, Paul 176
Trebanos 47, 50
Turner, Martin 52

Unlikely coup 179

Vardre RFC 50–1, 53–4

Ward, Ted 68
Warrington RLC 66, 177
Watkins, David 128, 160
Welsh Language/Culture 23–5, 114, 171–2
Welsh Sports Council 141
Western Mail 105, 118, 150, 182
West Wales League 50, 53, 96
White, Dai 74

Widnes RLC 177–8
Wigan RLC 67
Williams, Bleddyn 77, 79, 89, 112, 126, 153, 183
Williams, Gerwyn 153
Williams, Gwyn 76
Williams, J.J. 136, 160
Williams, J.P.R. 133, 160
Williams, Les 153
Williams, Lloyd 126–7
Williams, Nick 117
Williams, Ossie 142
Williams, Ray (Llanelli) 59, 68, 102
Williams, Rhys 143, 150
Williams, Sid 59
Willis, Rex 77, 96
World Cup 182
WRU 58–9, 117, 119, 127, 136, 140, 145, 154, 168–9, 173–9, 181